A Pyramid Gardening Paperback

# Organic
## garden basics

hamlyn

Bob Flowerdew

An Hachette UK Company
www.hachette.co.uk

A Pyramid Paperback

First published in Great Britain in 2007 by
Hamlyn, a division of Octopus Publishing Group Ltd
2–4 Heron Quays, London E14 4JP
www.octopusbooksusa.com

This edition published in 2010
Copyright © Octopus Publishing Group Limited
2007, 2008, 2010

Distributed in the U.S. and Canada by
Octopus Books USA:
c/o Hachette Book Group USA
237 Park Avenue
New York NY 10017

This material was previously published as *Go Organic!*

ISBN 978-0-600-62087-7

A CIP catalogue record for this book
is available from the British Library

Printed and bound in China

10 9 8 7 6 5 4 3 2 1

Left: Edible chrysanthemums and dill.

Right: The coneflower (Rudbeckia hirta).

# Contents

Introduction 4

Step 1: Improve your soil 6

Step 2: Make your own compost 22

Step 3: Avoid chemicals 30

Step 4: Choose the right plants 62

Step 5: Encourage wildlife 74

Grow organic 82

Planning an organic garden 124

A year in the garden 132

Index 140

Acknowledgments 144

# Introduction

Concerns about the pesticides, fungicides, insecticides, and other chemical sprays used in what is generally called "conventional" gardening and food production have made more and more of us question what it is, exactly, that we eat. When these anxieties are combined with an increased awareness of the damage, possibly irreparable, that we are doing to the environment, it is not surprising that many people nowadays are actively adopting organic principles in their gardens. If you grow your own vegetables, fruit, and herbs in an organic garden you know that they are free from the slightest taint of chemicals and that in growing them you have done nothing to harm the environment.

The aim of the organic gardener is to create an environment in which healthy plants can be grown successfully and pests and diseases discouraged without damaging or polluting the soil or destroying wildlife. Nature has created its own system of checks and balances, predators and prey, and if you create an environment in which they all flourish side by side, then nature will do much of the work for you.

The organic approach has been developed in response to the damage caused by conventional methods. Gardening (like commercial farming) has long been practiced as a form of warfare, in which crops are grown by doing battle with pests and diseases and by artificially stimulating their soil. Bad soil management, profligate use of chemicals, and overcropping have resulted in desertification and loss of productive land throughout the world and we are doing the same to our gardens.

## Organic principles

Protecting and increasing life in the soil is the first and most important principle of organic gardening. We are dependent on a healthy topsoil to feed us: if it becomes overworked it will erode and blow away, as has already happened on some overworked and overfarmed land. The only way to maintain, improve, and increase topsoil is by actively encouraging the multitude of microorganisms in the soil so that they can convert minerals and organic material into nutrients available for plant growth. It is these byproducts that build up water-retentive, loamy, humus-rich soil—the soil that promotes healthy plants. In return for short-term gains, using chemical fertilizers and overcropping burn off this store of nutrients and destroy the organisms.

Organic gardening works by feeding the soil, not the plants, and by using organic material instead of soluble chemicals. The burgeoning life in the soil uses this organic material, minerals, and the greater amounts of retained water to produce more life. Plants then feed on the byproducts, taking what they need to make their own growth.

The effect of adding organic material is cumulative: as more is introduced it encourages populations of soil flora and fauna. These larger populations support yet more life forms. So the variety and quantity of byproducts increases, raising the fertility of the soil. The plants living off this balanced diet are more healthy and resistant to pests and diseases than those living in denatured soil pumped up with cocktails of chemical fertilizers and kept going with poisonous sprays. To protect the life in the soil, organic gardeners use no poisonous substances that can harm them, apart from "natural" ones in the last resort. These are deemed to be acceptable because they are less wide-ranging in their toxicity and break down rapidly and naturally after use.

# Animals in the garden

The increasing life in an organic soil then goes on to support more and larger forms of life in the garden and surrounding environment. After all, if you want birds then you have to have worms. Again, the effects are cumulative. As more and larger forms of life come to the table of your soil they bring in minerals and nutrients, further enhancing its fertility. For example, birds shed feathers, eggshells, nesting material, copious droppings, and eventually their bodies, all of which contribute to the soil's fertility as they are broken down and reabsorbed into the chain of life.

Other creatures, such as frogs, toads, and chipmunks, take part in the same process, and all give off carbon dioxide, which is rapidly reabsorbed by garden plants. Few people realize how important this gas is for plant growth or that growing plants can extract all of it from still air in only minutes of bright sunlight. Animal life of any size in or on the soil gives off carbon dioxide and thus maintains growth.

Organic gardening also aims to mimic nature by increasing plant cover. In nature, bare soil soon disappears under a tangle of weeds, and in time tree and shrub seedlings turn it into dense woodland. All this growth increases the soil underneath while it fixes sunlight and extracts

*Above: The tayberry is a delicious loganberry variety with larger, sweeter fruits.*

more carbon dioxide from the air. Organic gardeners interplant between crops and use green manures before and after planting. These methods produce a natural soil cover that ensures soil stability, prevents wind and water erosion, and builds up the soil over time. The increased mixture and variety of plants not only aids pest and disease control but also improves the local ecology, providing a mini conservation area from which beneficial wildlife can move out to recolonize the local countryside.

The organic system further benefits the environment because it is far more self-sustaining, requiring less input. Home-grown fertility from green manures and compost replaces bought-in chemical fertilizers, and with subtler pest and disease control there is no need for direct intervention with ecologically damaging agrochemical pesticides.

Achieving an organic garden, improving your soil, recycling natural materials, avoiding chemicals, growing a wide range of plants, and attracting wildlife are all very simple, as this book proves.

# Step 1

# Improve your soil

Few people get the opportunity to choose the site or the soil for their gardens, and most of us have to make the best of what we've got. Many gardens are on old sites, which may be exhausted and pest-ridden. Some gardens are likely to be polluted and out of balance, especially if many chemicals have been used. On the other hand, abandoned or derelict sites, full of rampant weeds, will (unlikely as it seems) probably have good soil.

# Understanding your soil

Most soils will produce flowers, shrubs, or tree fruit without much improvement, but they will need more attention if you want to grow vegetables. Problem soils tend to be common to a particular locality, and it is always a good idea to see how your neighbors cope. Almost all soils can be easily improved, but it may be worth putting on extra topsoil if it is poor or polluted.

Most types of soil need the same basic treatment to improve them—that is, the addition of copious quantities of organic material. Anything else is almost inconsequential by comparison. However, although most soils can be improved and thus made acceptable to a wider range of plants, there is a difference between

improvement and change. It is hard to change the basic soil type, which determines what you can grow well, and it will make life easier if you accept what you've got rather than trying to modify it drastically. For example, trying to make an alkaline soil suitable for rhododendrons is futile; it is far better to grow philadelphus, fuchsias, cotoneasters, and other lime-lovers.

## Acidity and alkalinity

It is worth testing the acidity or alkalinity (lime content) of the soil, but do not use cheap meters, which are inaccurate. Simple chemical test kits with an accurate color chart are available in most garden stores. The basic pH may vary at ground level and further down if the soil layers have built up a rich surface mold, so take a number of samples from a typical worked soil. The pH may change as the soil is enriched, particularly as more organic material is added. This tends to make soils more acidic.

Adding lime to the soil every few years will be of benefit in most gardens, especially for vegetables and grassed areas. (Check if it is needed, though, because over-liming can cause its own problems.) Lime can take the form of chalk or, better, dolomitic lime, which contains more magnesium and other nutrients. Best of all is calcified seaweed, which contains all the trace elements as well as lime, although it can be rather slow-acting.

Never mix lime with manure or compost. Apply it before rain is expected on top of the soil or grass, and rake, brush, or allow it to leach in. Late winter is generally the best time. In a vegetable rotation it is probably best applied before peas or brassicas, but not before potatoes.

If, on the other hand, your soil is very alkaline, it may be lacking in available trace elements. To improve the soil you will need to use raised beds (see page 83) and dig in plenty of manure or compost.

# Soil amendments

Various materials are offered as soil amendments. Some flocculating agents based on lime or gypsum do help clay soils to form lighter textures, but most soils will benefit more from extra organic material, though builder's sand and grit will also help open up a heavy soil.

## Soil analysis

Analysis is unnecessary for most gardens, and you will get better value from a bag of seaweed meal. It is difficult to get accurate readings from the patchy soils in gardens, which can contain all sorts of detritus. If you aim to incorporate some broad-spectrum organic fertilizers and as much organic material as possible, most soils will balance themselves.

A more useful guide is to look at the plants that are growing well. For example, if your neighbors' gardens are full of flourishing rhododendrons, azaleas, and heathers, grow these plants too because the soil is obviously suitable, whatever the analysis says. Good gardeners grow what does well rather than coaxing unsuitable plants to grow in the wrong places.

*Above: Rhododendrons need an acidic soil to thrive, so if they grow in your garden you have acidic soil.*

# Soil types

All soils contain the same materials—stones, silt, sands, clays, and organic matter—but in varying proportions. What affects plants most is not the nutrient levels of the soil but its physical texture, aeration, and moisture retention. All (except peaty soils) will be improved considerably by adding more organic material, especially when it is combined with a mulch (see page 54).

Adding organic material contributes directly to the nutrient level and helps to increase another component of healthy soil: microorganisms. Mainly fungi, bacteria, and other microbes, these break down organic material to release further nutrients. These resources are then made available to the plants. In most soils, there is sufficient of almost every element to last for millions of years of heavy cropping—if microorganisms have the materials and conditions to thrive.

> Worms are probably the most important creatures in the garden

## Air and water

First of all, microorganisms need water, the most important factor for encouraging all life. Air is the next most important component. Almost all microlife and plant roots need oxygen and give off carbon dioxide. Much of the carbon dioxide is reabsorbed by the soil, but fresh air is needed to restore the oxygen content. Organic particles keep soils open and allow aeration.

## Soil composition

Soil composition varies with depth. Only the top 1in. (2.5cm) or so throbs with life, and this layer constitutes the most productive part of the soil. Keep it at its best by regularly adding an organic mulch to keep the soil warm, fed, and moist. At depths of more than 12in. (30cm), in the subsoil, only worms and plant roots live. The working depth of "living" soil is most efficiently maintained by their action alone: it is rarely practicable to dig to their depths. Digging may sometimes be necessary, but it disrupts the soil layers and should never bring up sterile subsoil.

## Encouraging worms

Worms are vital. Their casts have a granular texture which promotes root growth and their burrows act as aeration and drainage channels. The digestive process of worms reduces mineral particles in size, making them more accessible to microorganisms.

Encourage worms by keeping the soil moist and covered with a mulch. Fertilize bare soil and mulched areas with a handful of grass clippings every month or so as worms need "greens" as well as organic material, such as compost or well-rotted manure. Ground seaweed and other all-purpose fertilizers will also feed them. Rotary cultivating the soil will kill worms.

# Know your soil

| | Advantages | Disadvantages | Treatment |
|---|---|---|---|
| Heavy clay | • Rich soil • Rarely suffers from mineral deficiencies • Resists drought well • Good for fixed-bed gardening • Excellent for cauliflowers | • Hard to dig • Sticks to everything • Sets almost solid in dry weather • Drains poorly and pools with water in heavy rain • Encourages slugs | • Never allow to compact while wet • Add coarse organic material and builder's sand or grit • Will benefit from liming |
| Light, sandy soil | • Easy to dig • Washes off tools and shoes • Never pools with water • Warms earlier • Excellent for carrots if not too stony | • Loses humus quickly • Nutrients wash out easily • Dries out badly | • Add plenty of organic material, rock dusts (especially ground rock potassium) and organic fertilizers |
| Silt | • Fairly easily to dig • Good for most crops if well nourished | • Does not retain water • Tends to splash and crust badly in wet weather | • Add ground rock dusts |
| Peat | • High in organic material • Excellent for salad crops and soft fruits • Suits acid-loving plants (e.g. azaleas, some heathers) | • Sometimes short of nutrients • Dries out easily • Not stable enough for large trees • Good soil for weeds | • Add lime to broaden range of plants that can be grown |
| Loam | • Produced when old meadow or grass is dug up • Best because it encourages production of fine root hairs | • Hard to find • Possession encourages complacency | • Will need some annual organic material to maintain its fertility |
| Wet soil | • Although not suited to most crops, can be used to create magnificient ornamental gardens • Ideal for blueberries and cranberries | • Tends to be sour or acidic | • Add·large amounts of organic material to improve drainage and water dispersion • Add lime if necessary • Drain if low-lying |
| Alkaline soil | • Good for brassicas if also rich and moist • Good for many trees, figs, and grapes | • Causes chlorosis in acid-loving plants by locking up iron and other nutrients | • Add organic material and mulch plants for best results |
| Stony soil | • Tends to be free-draining • Best for permanent plantings rather than annuals and vegetables | • Difficult to hoe and cultivate | • Add thin layer of builder's sand to create workable soil |

# Drainage and digging

The aim of the organic gardener is to give plants the best conditions possible and to prevent them from ever coming under stress. Protection is needed from extremes of heat and cold and, most importantly, from water stress, which is most effectively achieved by increasing the organic matter and thus the humus content of the soil, which acts like a sponge, retaining moisture. However, too much water can be as bad as too little, so take care to get the balance right.

## Drainage

Waterlogging kills plants by driving out air. It is more of a problem on heavy soils, because the finer particles hold much more water than the coarse grains of sand or silt. It may be necessary to install a drainage system in the worst cases, but often breaking up compacted soil, encouraging earthworms with lime and mulches, applying organic material, and using raised beds will help the soil absorb the water, rather than just allowing it to drain away. If drainage is needed, ditches may work, or you may need to lay herringbones of drainage pipes leading to a French drain.

Clay soils retain more water than sandy or stony ones, which need much more watering in dry regions. It is the humus part of the soil that soaks up water, and so the higher the organic content the more water can be retained. Keep the soil moist, hoe the surface, or mulch and trap evaporation with layer upon layer of plants.

> Many gardens are run successfully without ever being dug

## Dig or no-dig

There has been much controversy over no-dig and digging methods, and both sides are partly right. The greater part of most gardens is no-dig anyway, and it is only the vegetable garden that gets dug regularly.

Certainly, digging a new area is a good idea, if only to unearth and remove trash and roots, but as an annual event it appears to be unproductive. The effort would be better spent on turning the compost pile or weeding, as any increase in yield

## Breaking new ground

At some time most of us want to make a new bed where none was before. The most important job is to remove all established weeds. Before embarking on the actual task it is a good idea to check that there are no pipes or wires under the ground and to dig carefully, as they may not be buried deep enough. Without doubt the easiest way to start a new bed is to put the whole area down to closely cut grass for a year or two and to cut the bed out of the turfgrass. It helps to be patient and plan ahead.

from digging is less than that obtained from one good watering at the right time for most crops.

Digging annually breaks up the natural soil layers, the network of earthworm tunnels and decaying root systems. It aerates the soil, causing excessive humus breakdown with a short-term increase in fertility, which may leach out if the digging precedes the crop by a long time. The need to produce a good seedbed does not justify digging unless the soil has been badly compacted; mulching and surface cultivation will make just as good a texture. However, most soils show benefit from a thorough digging once every five to ten years; if nothing else, this does destroy mole runs and ants' nests and the like. Many gardens are run successfully without ever being dug.

Digging benefits heavy soils more than lighter ones as frost may then help to break them down into a good crumb structure, but if badly dug it can just make lumps and air gaps. Light soil, which is easy to dig, needs it least.

No-dig methods mostly include permanent paths and fixed or raised beds so that the soil is not compacted by traffic. See also pages 82–3.

*Above: 'Early Onward' peas grown with corn and potatoes. Arranging plants close together helps to retain moisture in the soil.*

## Digging dos and don'ts

| Do | Don't |
|---|---|
| ✓ Pace yourself | ✗ Work for too long |
| ✓ Break each lump | ✗ Dig sodden soil |
| ✓ Mix in well-rotted manure as you go | ✗ Try to move too large a spadeful of soil |
| ✓ Dig heavy soils in drier fall weather | |
| ✓ Leave lighter soils until late winter so nutrients don't leach out | |

# Soil fertility

You get better results with almost any plant from a deep, rich, moist soil full of organic material, so every effort should be made to amend the soil before planting. Needless to say, it will be much more difficult later on. All poor sites will need building up with copious quantities of organic material before you can even think about planting.

## Maintaining soil fertility

In general, if you regularly feed your soil with well-rotted manure and compost, it will remain fertile. In addition, the rotation of crops in the vegetable garden leaves root and leaf residues, and this will be increased if green manures are grown between crops and then hoed or dug in (see pages 18–20). Regular feeding of the plants as such does not take place in an organic system, but the soil is fed with plant residues as well as compost or well-rotted farmyard manure mixed in whenever a heavy feeder or perennial is planted.

Environmentally concerned gardeners will avoid using peat extracted from peat bogs

Mulches of organic material break down and are soon incorporated. Rock dusts, especially potassium, can be added with benefit at any time, but take several seasons to act. Ground rock dusts provide additional raw materials of the most needed elements in a finely distributed form and benefit most soils, especially lighter ones. For poor soils in the first few years, some supplementary feeding may be undertaken with organic fertilizers of a faster-acting nature. These are crutches, and should be discarded as the soil becomes enriched. Far more important for fertility is ensuring that the life in the soil is active; mulching and keeping the soil moist helps most.

## Peat

Peat is partly decomposed plant material that accumulates in bogs at a very slow rate, so it is theoretically a sustainable resource. But it is currently extracted on a profligate industrial scale from irreplaceable sites of scientific and wildlife significance. Environmentally concerned gardeners will avoid using peat extracted from bogs, though that from reservoir bottoms may be acceptable. In any case peat makes a poor mulch as it is too fine; much better alternatives are composted manures, shredded bark and wood wastes (see page 57).

Peat also has very little fertility value and it is really best reserved for specialty potting mixes, especially for acid-loving (effectively meaning "peat-loving") plants. In most other potting mixes peat is not as desirable as leafmold or good loam. Soilless (loam-free) potting mixes are popular as they are light and easy to use but the peat they contain most often comes from nonrenewable sources. There are now many good, alternative growing mediums, including those based on coir, bark, crop residues and even, in some areas, composted municipal waste.

# Peat-free sowing and potting mix ingredients

| Ingredient | Advantages | Disadvantages |
|---|---|---|
| Coir | • Widely available • Effective • Free of weed seeds | • Easy to water badly |
| Composted bark | • Effective • Free of weed seeds • Good ecologically | • Easy to water badly |
| Composted crop wastes | • Effective • Free of weed seeds • Good ecologically | • Easy to water badly • Potential residues |
| Leafmold | • Superb • Roots love it | • Not free of weed seeds • Hard to get good quality in quantity |
| Loam (rotted down sods) | • Effective • Heavy • Roots love it | • Not free of weed seeds • Hard to buy good quality |
| Sifted garden compost | • Effective • Heavy • Rich in nutrients | Full of weed seeds Impossible to buy |
| Well-rotted manure | • Effective • Available in quantity • Rich in nutrients | • Not free of disease or weed seeds • Easy to water badly • Potential residues |
| Composted municipal wastes | • Effective • Available in quantity • Some nutrients | • Potentially full of residues |
| Builder's sand and grit | • Widely available • Cheap • Superb drainage | • No nutrient- or water-holding value • Needs mixing with others |

# Fertilizers, liquid feeds, and manures

## Fertilizers

Conventional fertilizers are ranked according to the relative proportions of nitrogen, phosphorus, and potassium they contain. They are regarded as direct plant foods, replacing the elements taken away with the crops. Nitrogen (N) is considered to stimulate leafy growth, phosphorus (P) to feed roots, and potassium (K) to promote fruiting and increase disease resistance. These elements exist naturally in the soil, but it is not natural to have them in high concentrations, as occurs when they are applied as soluble fertilizers.

Organic gardeners protect the microorganisms in the soil by avoiding substances that can damage them; instead, they use fertilizers that are effectively insoluble so they cannot become too concentrated in the soil solution. These fertilizers need to be broken down and incorporated by microorganisms before they can increase the nutrient supply in the soil and become available to plants. Thus they do not leach out as readily, and remain beneficial for longer.

> Organic gardeners protect the micro-organisms in the soil by avoiding substances that can damage them

Organic fertilizers may, therefore, be considered more as soil stimulators than as plant fertilizers as they promote increases in soil life, and the byproducts from this increased population then feed the plants. Because they are stimulators or catalysts, they do not need to be applied in large quantities. A handful per square yard (meter) every other year is usually sufficient.

Note that blood, fish and bone meal, bone meal and hoof and horn are ethically dubious, and likely to be taken by animals or birds unless they are mixed in well with the soil; keep the bags in a safe place.

### Seaweed meal

This contains a wide spread of trace elements and 2–3 percent each of nitrogen and potassium, but only a sixth as much phosphate. The most widely acceptable nitrogenous fertilizer and soil stimulator, seaweed meal is also a good compost activator.

It is more pleasant to use and more acceptable ecologically than blood, fish and bone meal for a general-purpose feed. It is expensive but long-lasting, and it is better balanced when mixed with bone meal or ground rock phosphate, but is effective enough on its own for most plants. It should be raked into the soil in spring.

### Blood, fish and bone meal

This traditional, organically based fertilizer is both effective and fast-acting, and should be used in moderation. Rake it in immediately before planting hungry feeders or mix it with the planting soil. Beware of cheap brands, however, which are frequently adulterated with chemical fertilizers and sand.

## Bone meal

An excellent source of phosphates, bone meal acts most quickly in fine soil. Although expensive, it is good for incorporating in the soil when planting, particularly woody plants and strawberries.

## Hoof and horn

Although expensive, hoof and horn is an effective slow-release source of nitrogen for hungry and woody plants.

# Calcified seaweed

This fertilizer is more of a lime than a fertilizer, but because of its high level of trace elements it may act like a fertilizer by stimulating soil life. It is considerably cheaper than seaweed and may, therefore, be used as an all-purpose fertilizer where the lime will be no disadvantage. Calcified seaweed is especially beneficial for turfgrass, brassicas, legumes, and stone fruits.

### Ground rock potassium

This is exactly what its name suggests: a ground rock dust. It releases potassium slowly and is best used by being mixed in composts or into the soil at any time every two or three years, particularly

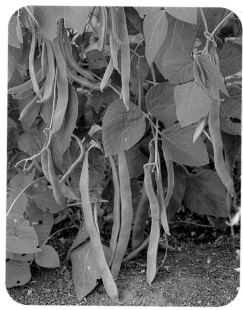

*Above: 'Cambridge Vigour' strawberries in midsummer ready for picking. Strawberries benefit from having bone meal incorporated into the soil at planting time.*

*Above: Runner beans, like all leguminous plants, will benefit from an application of calcified seaweed, which contains high levels of trace elements.*

on light soils and in wet areas. It is especially good for gooseberries and culinary apples and for promoting disease resistance in plants.

### Ground rock phosphate

This rock dust is useful for restoring healthy life to abused or overacidic soils, especially in wet areas. Mix it in composts or in the soil at any time. It is especially good for strawberries.

### Ground rock basalt or granite

This finely ground rock dust, which may also be added to any soil, contains a spread of minerals to encourage microorganisms and is claimed to revitalize worn-out soils.

### Wood ash

Wood ashes are a rich source of potassium, but it is in a soluble form which leaches out of the soil. The ash should, therefore, be applied to growing crops, especially fruit and onions, for ripening and disease protection. Sprinkle on the surface and rake in or add to the compost pile.

### Commercial balanced "organic" fertilizers

These commercial preparations are usually expensive. Most are based on animal wastes, which have been composted or worm composted. They may be contaminated with diseases and residues, so only those with the Soil Association or similar symbol can be recommended.

### Sewage sludge

Because this, too, is likely to be contaminated, it can be recommended only for ornamental plantings where it is a slow-release source of phosphate. Avoid using in vegetable gardens.

# Liquid fertilizers

Plants confined in containers are restricted and cannot reach farther afield for nutrients after they have used up those around the rootball. They need feeding little and often with a liquid fertilizer diluted in their water. These liquid feeds may smell unpleasant, but this disappears when they are absorbed into the soil. All the fertilizers discussed below are for plants with restricted root runs, though they may be used in moderation on hungry plants in the open such as corn.

### Comfrey liquid

Comfrey leaves are collected, packed into a container (such as a rain barrel), activated with a little urine, and covered in water. They rot down in four to five weeks to form a solution like black tea. It smells horrible, but watered down to a pale straw color is a perfectly balanced feed for tomatoes and other plants. Another method is to stack the leaves in a covered container with a hole in the base, and leave them to rot down without added liquid. After a few weeks a liquid concentrate will start to drip out. This again can be diluted and used as a liquid feed. The concentrate can also be used as the fertility constituent in potting mixes.

### Nettle tea

This is made and used in the same way as comfrey liquid, but with fertilizer nettles instead. As well as being a good balanced fertilizer, it is claimed to make plants more resistant to diseases and pests. Similarly, bags of manure can be hung in sacks in rain barrels and the resulting solution used in the same way as nettle tea.

### Seaweed solution

Diluted down and used as a beneficial liquid feed, this carries the benefits of a wider range of trace elements, but is expensive to use for general watering and should be saved for use as a foliar feed. The effect on plants is rapid and marked. They take on a darker, healthier color and resist pests and diseases better.

### Fish emulsion

A rich source of nutrients, this is especially effective when it is mixed with seaweed solution and applied as a liquid feed.

# Animal manures

Manure is probably the best soil improver of all, but you have to take what you can get and that from intensive rearing units may contain unacceptable residues. All animal manures make a contribution to soil fertility, but they should always be well composted before use. This will help to get rid of some chemical contaminants. Avoid manures from farms that use intensive rearing methods as there will be contaminants from the feed or from drugs or hormones administered to the animals—pig and poultry manure from intensive farms should be particularly avoided. The straw or wood shavings the manures come in may themselves be polluted.

> One barrow-load of manure will muck 12 square yards (10 square meters)

*Above: Comfrey liquid is a cheap and effective liquid feed which can be made at home using comfrey leaves. Nettle tea is made in the same way.*

Stack the manure in a pile, cover it to protect it from the rain, and leave for a year if possible. As a rule, one barrow-load of manure will feed 12 square yards (10 square meters).

In order of preference, horse, sheep, and goat manures are all sweet to handle; cow manure is less pleasant; pig manure is vile and often contains unacceptable contaminants. Rabbit and pet droppings can be added to the compost pile, but cat and dog tray litter is best buried under trees. Poultry manures are strong, highly nitrogenous and a good source of potassium. They make a compost pile cook! Never put raw poultry droppings on plants; always compost them first.

### Mushroom compost

Nonorganic mushroom compost should be avoided as it is also likely to be contaminated with persistent and undesirable chemicals.

# Green manures

Any plants that are grown as temporary groundcover and are then dug into the soil as fertilizer are known as green manures, although in some cases the tops of the plants may be cut and composted for use elsewhere. They are usually grown over winter when the soil is vacant, but may also be grown between crops and incorporated as seedlings after only a week or two. They prevent soil erosion and leaching and convert otherwise wasted winter sunlight into useful organic plant matter.

Any plants that grow over winter will do, but those that are easiest to incorporate or that create most bulk are best. Leguminous plants,

## Green manures

| Manure | Advantages | Disadvantages |
|---|---|---|
| Alfalfa (lucerne) | • Deep-rooting and pulls up minerals from 20ft. (6m) | • Slow-growing • For nitrogen-fixing, soil must be treated with *Rhizobium* bacteria (sold with seed) |
| Beans and peas | • Any variety suitable, but only hardy ones will overwinter | • Crop rotation is important when used in vegetable garden |
| Buckwheat | • Grows quickly in late spring/early summer • Can be left to flower as it is good for beneficial insects • Deep roots and will choke out most weeds | • Not nitrogen-fixing • Must be removed before it sets seed |
| Clover | • Rich source of nitrogen • Good for bees if allowed to flower | • Needs a year or so to show full benefit • Inclined to regrow |
| Chicory | | • Long-term plant, best used in grass and clover pastures as it has deep taproots that take time to form (and kill) |
| Fenugreek | • Nitrogen-fixing • Quick-growing and suitable for use after early crops or between others • Unrelated to vegetables and so no problem with rotation • Can be sown late spring to late summer but is killed by first frosts | |

# Green manures

| Manure | Advantages | Disadvantages |
|---|---|---|
| Fodder radish | • Killed by hard frosts, leaving considerable bulk, which can be easily incorporated into the soil in spring | • Related to brassicas so must be used sparingly in rotations including these crops • Hard to dig in |
| Hungarian grazing rye | • Sow from late summer to midfall for quick groundcover for overwintering | • Not nitrogen fixing • Very hard to dig in and this must be done a month before the crop to allow time for rotting |
| *Limnanthes douglasii* | • Good for producing bulk and suppressing weeds • Sown late summer or fall it will overwinter • Good for beneficial insects if left | • No drawbacks |
| Lupines | • Nitrogen-fixing • Deep-rooted • Sown in spring and incorporated in fall, will help to improve sour, acidic land | • Agricultural forms are better than ordinary garden lupines |
| Mustard | • Fast-growing • When incorporated as seedlings can reduce many infestations of the soil • Best grown between crops or up until the frosts and incorporated *in situ* | • Not nitrogen-fixing • In the brassica family and must be grown with care in rotations; ideally only to the seedling stage • Will not withstand hard winters |
| *Phacelia tanacetifolia* | • Attracts bees and flower flies • Sown in early spring to early fall, it may overwinter • Easy to remove from the soil or to incorporate in it | • Not nitrogen fixing • Seed is expensive (but can be saved) |
| Trefoil | • A nitrogen-fixing legume, similar to clover and related to alfalfa • Tolerates shade so can be grown beneath taller crops • Sow from early spring to late fall and will overwinter | • Prefers alkaline soil |
| *Valerianella* (corn salad) | • Good for producing bulk and suppressing weeds • Sow late summer or fall for overwintering • Edible | • No drawbacks |
| Winter tares | • Good for producing bulk and suppressing weeds • Nitrogen-fixing • Can be sown from early spring to late fall for overwintering | • Hard to dig in |

*Above: Buckwheat is an excellent, fast-growing green manure. Remove or dig in the plants before they can set seed.*

*Above:* Limnanthes douglasii *is a good choice as a green manure as it both suppresses weeds and creates bulk.*

which fix nitrogen, are frequently used because this nutrient is always in short supply. The manures are usually sown as soon as the ground is bare and until the first frosts start. Those surviving over winter are killed off by impenetrable mulches or are dug in before the crops need the soil. Several weeks of breakdown are necessary for some of the more fibrous green manures, such as grazing rye, but less time is needed for younger and more succulent growth.

Never let green manures flower and go to seed or the goodness will be lost from the plants. In general, too, it is better to grow two or three short crops than one long-lasting one.

Peas and beans are removed minus their roots before they form pods, leaving nitrogen-rich nodules in the soil. 'Banner' is a hardy variety of fava (field) bean, which is often grown as a green manure. 'Alsike' is the best clover for poor, wet, or acidic soils, while white clover is better on lighter and limier soils. 'Essex Red' is considered the best clover for green manuring, although it is not reliably hardy and does better on loamy soils.

> Never let green manures flower and go to seed

# Minerals

Some garden plants and many weeds are particularly good at accumulating large amounts of minerals and trace elements. In fact, these plants often abound on deficient soils because they are the most successful at grabbing scarce resources. Nettles, for example, indicate that the soil is rich in phosphorus, but clover grows best on soil that is deficient in nitrogen. Although these plants extract most of the nutrients, more will be dissolved into the soil from otherwise insoluble mineral sources. Growing these plants as green manures removes scarce minerals, but once they are composted the concentrated material can be put back to boost the soil. Remember that only annual weeds should be used as green manure as perennial weeds are hard to eradicate.

## Mineral accumulators

| Mineral | Benefits | Source |
| --- | --- | --- |
| Calcium | Promotes development of plant cell walls | Concentrated by buckwheat, corn marigold, dandelion, goosegrass, lamb's quarters, *Matricaria recutita* (German chamomile), melons, purslane, and shepherd's purse |
| Nitrogen | Promotes healthy foliage | Taken from the air (not the soil) and best accumulated with leguminous plants and by digging in any succulent seedlings in their first flushes of growth |
| Phosphorus | Promotes healthy root development | Concentrated by corn marigold, lamb's quarters, purslane, vetches, and the weed *Datura stramonium* (jimsonweed) |
| Potassium | Promotes formation of flowers and fruit | Accumulated by several plants, including chickweed, chicory, goosegrass, jimsonweed, lamb's quarters, plantain, purslane, flowering tobaccos, and vetches |
| Silica | Promotes disease resistance | Made active by *Equisetum* (horsetails) plantains, quackgrass, and stinging nettles |
| Sulfur | Promotes disease resistance | Accumulates in *Allium* (onion), brassicas, lamb's quarters, and purslane |

# Step 2

# Make your own compost

Making your own compost brings a number of benefits: it avoids wastage, is cost-efficient, and gives you the confidence that no unwanted chemicals, pests, or diseases are present. As long as you bear in mind a few simple rules, it is not difficult and can be immensely satisfying.

## About compost

Composting is the accelerated rotting down of once-living things. It converts waste into a brown, soillike mass that is pleasant to smell and use. This mass is almost pure plant food and is in a form readily available to plant roots with no risk of the overfeeding or imbalance that can be caused by chemical fertilizers. Moreover, the vast number of different microorganisms that have broken down the compost go on to colonize the soil once the compost is added, further aiding fertility.

> Siftings from previous compost piles are the best activator of all

All manures and other organic materials for use in the garden are better composted before use, except clean commercial mulching materials and clean straw. Fresh manures contain soluble nutrients, which can be too strong for healthy growth, but if they are stacked and turned they compost. Once composted, their fertility is less easily lost and they become safer for plant roots. This is why it is always recommended that only well-rotted animal manure is used. Because of the variety of materials going into a compost pile, garden compost contains a greater spread of nutrients and more varied microlife than well-rotted manure, so it is used in preference.

As the composting process converts most of the nutrients into an insoluble form there is little danger of their washing out into the water table in heavy rainfall. However, they do leach out slowly, so compost piles and rotting manures should always be covered.

# Troubleshooting

| Problem | Action |
| --- | --- |
| Too wet | Remake with extra straw or dry material |
| Too dry | Add water, fresh wet manure, or grass clippings to the pile |
| Dry with white coating on material | Add water mixed with urine to add liquid and nitrogen |

## Making compost

There are many different ways of composting, but they all come back to one principle.

• In general, composting proceeds best when there are many, varied materials, well divided, moistened, and thoroughly mixed together with plentiful air.

## When to use compost

Fresh compost, even when immature, can be mixed into the soil when you are planting trees and shrubs, but if it is to be used as a topdressing or with small plants, such as when planting out cabbages, it is best used matured and sifted. This takes extra effort but produces a finer material, and the residue can then be used to start the next pile. In any case, compost or well-rotted manure is best applied to growing crops in early spring, so that the nutrients are taken up rather than leaching out of the soil over the winter months.

• It helps to have roughly equal amounts of dry material and fresh green material as too much of either will cause poor composting.

• Adding water when mixing is usually necessary as many materials are too dry on their own.

• An activator is not essential, but speeds things up if added during the mixing. Rather than chemical additives it is better to use urine or poultry manure. Seaweed or blood, fish and bone meal will do instead. Siftings from previous compost piles are the best activator of all, and, if you are starting your first pile, try to get some from a more experienced gardener to mix in.

## Covering the pile

Keeping the rain out and the heat in the pile is usually best done with a plastic sheet or two and some insulation such as bubble wrap or carpet laid over the pile. The sides of the pile should also be insulated in cold weather, but they are best made open to allow air in and out as the pile matures. The top of the compost pile must stay covered to dry the pile out ready for sifting and to prevent some of the nutrients leaching out.

*Above: Wooden compost containers allow the air to circulate around all sides of the pile. Many, like this one, have removable slats at the front for easy access.*

## To turn or not

It is always better to turn and remix the compost pile; the more the better, especially if the pile is small. Extra grass clippings, urine, and dung can be added at this stage to make it cook properly if it is poor stuff. If the compost appears to be wet and slimy, mix in some torn-up paper or unglazed cardboard. Having a bin on a stand makes turning out potentially easier but filling harder work. Rotary composters only work well with soft materials.

## How long?

If insulated and mixed well with only soft and green materials, a pile can be ready in less than a month in summer. If made by slow accumulation in layers in a badly insulated bin, then it will take about three years.

## Maturing the pile

I like to plunge a crowbar down into the center of my pile once it is going. It has little effect, but I love to pull it out and watch it steam, showing me the pile is cooking well. Once the pile has been turned and cooked at least twice it is left to mature for six months, when it is ready for use. If you leave it longer, the worms mineralize it, increasing its richness but decreasing the quantity. It makes excellent potting mix, albeit containing some weed seeds.

## Small composters

|  | Advantages | Disadvantages |
|---|---|---|
| Plastic | Often free or subsidized<br>Easy to assemble and use | Usually too small and poorly insulated<br>Ecologically dubious<br>Aesthetically grim |
| Wood | More aesthetic<br>Easy to make at home | Expensive, as it will rot in a few years<br>Too small and too poorly insulated |

# Compost containers

Several different styles of compost containers are sold, but most are on the small side and thus do not heat up enough to make really good compost unless given extra insulation.

Simple constructions of wood, wire netting, or brick, about 3ft. (1m) in height, width, and depth are sufficient, and considerably cheaper. I prefer to use old wooden fencing tied at the corners. This is easily obtained. Do not paint the compost bin with preservative as this will slow the process. A lid will keep out the rain, but an old carpet and a plastic sheet will be better for retaining the heat and will prevent a flush of weeds from growing on top.

## In a small garden

In a small garden a compost bin or a container is more suitable than a straggly, untidy pile of the kind that can be tucked away at the bottom of a largish garden. Make your own container from a square cage of wire netting supported by four stout posts driven into the ground. Ideally, make the front removable so that you can easily get to the rotted compost inside.

Traditional bins made from slatted wood will keep the compost looking tidy. They can be easily made from timber boards or fencing, or you can buy wood that is already cut to length that slots neatly together. Some of the better composters are supplied with wooden tops; otherwise, remember to cover the full bin with old carpet and plastic to keep in the heat and stop the rain getting into the compost.

Cone-shaped, black or dark green plastic composters, which hold from 8–10 cu ft. (220–300 liters) or more, are a tidy and convenient alternative to a pile. In a small garden the problem is often that there is insufficient waste material to allow a sufficiently large pile to build up, so the material never gets hot enough to begin to break down. You will get far better results with two smallish bins: fill one and leave it for a time or, better, mix and turn it into the second, additionally insulated, leave to cook and mature while you begin to fill up the first bin again.

> Composting slows if the bin is painted with preservative

## Instant containers

Convert a dead fridge or small freezer into a hot composting container with some gutter sealant and black bituminous paint. The super-insulated container keeps the compost much hotter and works amazingly well if the ingredients are emptied and remixed with plenty of air worked in. It runs wetter and, unless dryish material is mixed in, an ooze accumulates which can then be tapped off and diluted for use as a liquid feed.

# Materials for composting

The composting process will rapidly break down almost all natural materials, including old clothes made of natural fibers and wetted newspaper. Large lumps of wood, bone, or fat will decay too slowly and should be broken up or buried. Dry, twiggy material will compost if chopped up and mixed with some nitrogenous material, such as fresh manure. Thorny material is better discarded, material containing seeds is best put in the middle of a pile, and live weeds of a pernicious nature can be killed first by wilting them on a path or sheet of plastic before mixing them in. Alternatively such weeds and seeds can first be drowned for a month or two in a rain barrel before adding them to the compost pile. Diseased material may be composted, but only if you are confident that your heap will "cook" well; otherwise it is safer to discard it.

## Leafmold

The leaves of deciduous trees and shrubs can be rotted down on their own to make soil-enriching leafmold.

A simple wire container, made from chicken wire stretched between four upright posts that have been driven into the ground, makes a suitable leafmold bin.

A fast, space-saving alternative is to pack the layers of leaves into black plastic garbage bags that have been perforated to allow in air. Filled and tied at the top, the bags should be stood in an out-of-the-way corner until the following spring, by when the contents, gathered the previous fall, will have turned into good leafmold. Leaves that are kept in outdoor bins may take longer to break down.

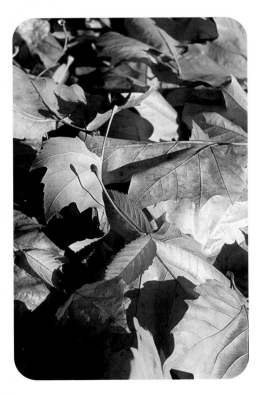

*Below: Rake up leaves in fall and rot them down to make leafmold or you can add them to the compost pile.*

# Compost materials

Note that glass, plastic, and metal will not break down and should not be added to your compost pile.

| Materials | Speed of composting | Notes |
|---|---|---|
| Bedding plants | Slow | |
| Bracken | Intermediate | Do not use when spores are visible |
| Cardboard | Slow | |
| Comfrey leaves | Fast | A good activator |
| Flowers | Intermediate | |
| Fruit and vegetable scraps | Intermediate | |
| Grass clippings | Fast | Mix in well to avoid "crusting" |
| Hedge clippings (soft) | Intermediate | Valuable for minerals |
| Hedge clippings (woody) | Slow | Chop or shred before adding |
| Herbaceous plants | Intermediate | |
| Leaves (deciduous) | Slow | |
| Nettles | Fast | A good activator |
| Newspaper | Slow | Soaks up liquids |
| Poultry manure | Fast | High in nitrogen |
| Rhubarb leaves | Intermediate | |
| Seaweed | Fast | Adds trace elements and encourages bacterial breakdown |
| Straw (old) | Slow | Soak thoroughly if dry |
| Straw-based animal manure | Intermediate | Valuable fertility in this |
| Tea and coffee grounds | Intermediate | |
| Tea bags | Intermediate | |
| Vegetable stems (tough) | Intermediate | Cut into small pieces |
| Weeds, annual | Fast | Only add seeds if pile will get hot enough to kill them |
| Weeds, perennial | Intermediate | Kill weeds before adding to pile |

Weeds and seeds can be drowned for a month or two in a rain barrel before adding to the compost pile

gallons of water to flush such a rich source of fertility into the sea.

Saved in a bucket, it makes a superb compost activator; alternatively, each day's quota can be diluted down about 20:1 and watered on last thing at night to feed lawns and increase the cuttings for use elsewhere.

*Below: Leaves layered into black plastic garbage bags and then left for several months will turn into an enriching leafmold.*

*Above: Nettles have many positive qualities: they attract beneficial insects to the garden and they compost quickly too.*

Although some people are squeamish, it is sensible to recycle urine if local regulations do not forbid it. This is not a health hazard in temperate climates, and it is wasteful to use a couple of

# Easy composting

Perhaps the biggest drawback to effective composting is the problem of accumulating enough material to make an effective pile—the bigger the mass the more heat is retained and the better it composts.

Rather than store material until enough is available, I spread mine on the ground for the hens to rummage through, and their feet pack it down. Later I scrape it up and put it in the bins to break down. If you don't have hens, it is probably best kept in garbage bags until ready to be combined, but most people just put it in layers in a bin and dig it out and mix it when enough has built up.

A pile will always make better compost if it is remade after a week and the inside exchanged for the outside. Doing this again after another week will be of further benefit. Each turning mixes the ingredients and stirs in air which then speeds up the process. Do not pack a pile down as this has the opposite effect. There are commercial rotary composters which speed up the process, but these are better suited to warm-climate regions.

Where there is little material available at any time, there are alternatives to the conventional pile. Cooperation with several neighbors can allow each to make a pile in turn or to share in yours. Another method is pit composting. Dig a hole and put the compost material in, covering each layer with a thin layer of soil. Once the hole is full and proud start another and use the first for growing really hungry feeders on, such as squash, pole beans, or potatoes, for a year or two. The pit can then be dug out and the rotted material used as compost.

## Worm compost

Making worm compost is an ideal way of using up household garbage in winter when material rots down slowly on the compost pile because of the cold. The waste has to be chopped up finely and added a little at a time to a large container containing red brandling worms. (You can buy these or unearth them from a manure or compost pile, or from under a wooden board or carpet laid on the ground.)

Put the worms in a layer of moist peat or leafmold in the bottom of the container and keep in the warm (in the basement, for example). The container should have air holes in the top, and drainage holes and a drip tray to catch any liquids that ooze out. This liquid makes a good feed when diluted. The worms convert the vegetable waste to a rich material that is best mixed in when planting hungry feeders or that can be added to potting mixes.

The worms will die if dug out with the material and put in the soil, so carefully sift them and return them to the container. The worms will not deal with a large quantity of matter at a time, so they are better for small households or for use in conjunction with another container or with a conventional compost pile. Avoid large amounts of citrus peel and dairy produce.

The conventional solution to pests and diseases relies heavily on sprays, which drench plants and soil with chemical poisons. Organic gardeners try instead to help plants to resist attacks in the first place by manipulating the natural system of checks and balances in their favor. Pesticides, even organic ones, are used only as a last resort.

# Controlling pests and diseases

The aim of the organic gardener is control, not elimination. The gardener makes life difficult for pests and diseases so that plants and crops thrive in spite of them. Organic gardeners aim to prevent pests and diseases from reaching the point where an organically approved pesticide might be needed by building up a wide variety of plants, by creating stable ecosystems and by encouraging predators and parasites.

## Growing healthy plants

The primary task in organic gardening is to grow healthy plants that resist attacks and endure minor infestations in much the same way that healthy humans shrug off a cold.

Of all the checks to growth, water imbalance is probably the most common. Desiccated plants will die, but if they even reach wilt point their growth will be severely checked. Waterlogging can be equally serious, especially in cold, low-light conditions. Plants in containers are as often sickened by overwatering in winter and spring as they are by drought in summer.

Air and light are also important factors in preventing infection: each plant must be given

> The aim of the organic gardener is control, not elimination

# Organic pesticides

Organic gardeners prefer not to use poisonous substances unless they are needed to save a valuable crop. However, they are there as a last resort, though you must take great care not to disrupt ecosystems that have slowly built up. Follow the instructions on the packaging as to their uses, application rates and timing, and precautions, and keep them in a safe place.

| Pesticides | Advantages | Disadvantages |
|---|---|---|
| Bordeaux mixture | • An inorganic chemical allowed under organic standards as it is not harmful to humans or soil life • Effective against potato blight, peach leaf curl, raspberry cane spot, and many other fungal diseases | • It is a preventative, not a cure, and must be applied thoroughly and in good time |
| Derris | • Liquid or dust, which kills most insects, but is particularly effective against mites • Treat wasps' nests by puffing the dust into the entrance at dusk; repeat after a week | • Indiscriminate in action • Lethal to fish, pigs, and tortoises • Breaks down in sunlight • Slower to act than pyrethrum • Currently under review and no longer recommended for use in some places |
| Insecticidal soap | • The preferred pesticide and even more effective than soft soap • Safe to use and made from natural products | • Ineffective against larger insect pests |
| Pyrethrum | • Useful for killing many insect pests, including small caterpillars | • No longer available in pure form and commonly supplied with a synthetic synergist • Kills beneficial insects and fish (but is safe for mammals) |
| Quassia | • Solution (made from a tree bark) that kills aphids but is harmless to bees and other beneficial insects • Sold combined with derris, which makes both more effective | • No longer available on its own |
| Soft soap | • Traditionally used as a spray to kill aphids, red spider mites, mealy bugs, whiteflies, and other pests | |
| Sulfur | • The pure element is allowed under organic standards as a control for powdery mildews on fruit, flowers, and vegetables and for preventing rots in overwintering bulbs and tubers | • Take care when using it with fruit trees and bushes as a few varieties are allergic to sulfur • Read the label and instructions |

sufficient space. Never crowd plants—grow a few well rather than many poorly. Vigorous and woody plants need pruning or tying in to allow in air and light, and to allow access for useful predators.

## Hygiene

Regular inspection of all parts of the garden, followed by prompt action to remove infected material, will significantly reduce further pest

*Below: A cluster of sempervivums flower in front of golden feverfew, flowering parsley, and rosemary. Decorative herbs can be mixed with ornamentals.*

and disease attacks. For example, the removal of any infested tips controls aphid attacks on fava beans and the prompt removal and deep burial of infected branches prevents the spread of coral spot. Pruners, saws, and knives should be sterilized with surgical spirit to prevent cross-infection occurring.

Take care not to introduce any problems with bought-in plants, manures, or dirty tools. Keep new plants in isolation for a week or two. Never buy soil-grown brassica plants because of the danger of clubroot.

There is no need to become overfastidious with hygiene, however: a small level of pest infestation is necessary to maintain predator populations. It is a good idea to keep things in proportion: the prime cause of loss in the garden is bad weather. Bad practices, such as overcrowding and poor weed control, come a close second. Pests come third, with birds worst of all. Most other pests and diseases are far less common or troublesome.

## Direct action

In addition to building self-regulating systems, you will occasionally need to take direct action—and the earlier that action is taken the more effective it will be.

What must also be considered is the economics, in time, cash, and labor, of any measure you take in relation to the increase in yield. For example, flea beetles make shot holes in radish and brassica seedlings: maintaining moist conditions reduces their damage and is worthwhile, but spraying may cost more than a radish crop is worth.

# Basics of biological control

Bought-in predators have been used commercially for some time, and many are now available to gardeners. Many pests can be controlled by sprinkling on a water-borne parasite, usually a microscopic worm called a nematode; the soil needs to be moist and warm for this to work. For example, soil weevils can be parasitized by *Steinernema feltiae* nematodes applied to soil in summer. Most biological controls are more suitable for greenhouses, where pests are difficult to control because of the absence of natural predators. Once they are introduced, of course, the use of pesticides has to stop. They are most effective if introduced early in the season, but not before the pest has appeared or the parasites will starve. Full instructions come in the packets.

Most widely used are the controls for whiteflies, spider mites, aphids, and mealybugs.

## Biological controls

| Pest | Control |
|------|---------|
| Aphids | **Greenhouse:** Once the temperature is above 50°F (10°C) introduce *Aphidoletes aphidomyza* (predatory midge) or *Aphidius* (parasitic wasp)<br>**Garden:** Tap lacewing larvae onto infected plants<br>Introduce lacewing "hotel" for overwintering |
| Caterpillars | **Greenhouse:** Introduce *Bacillus thuringiensis* (bacterium) in the evening |
| Fungus gnat | **Greenhouse:** Introduce *Hypoaspis miles* (predatory mite) when the temperature is above 52°F (11°C) |
| Mealybugs | **Greenhouse:** Introduce *Cryptolaemus montrouzieri* (predatory ladybeetle) on large plants and *Hypoaspis miles* (predatory mite) on small plants when the temperature is above 52°F (11°C) |
| Scale insects | **Greenhouse:** When the temperature is above 57°F (14°C) introduce *Steinernema* (nematode) or *Metaphycus helvolus* (parasitic wasp) |
| Slugs | **Greenhouse:** When the soil temperature is above 41°F (5°C) apply *Phasmarhabditis hermaphrodita* (pathogenic nematode) every six weeks |
| Spider mites | **Greenhouse:** If the temperature is above 61°F (16°C) introduce *Phytoseiulus persimilis* (predatory mite) at first sign of infestation |
| Thrips | **Greenhouse:** Introduce *Ambleysius* (predatory mite) from late spring |
| Vine weevils | **Greenhouse:** When the soil temperature is over 54°F (12°C) apply *Heterorhabditis megidis* or *Steinernema carpocapsae* (pathogenic nematodes)<br>**Garden:** When the soil temperature is over 54°F (12°C) apply pathogenic nematodes |
| Whiteflies | **Greenhouse:** Once the temperature is above 50°F (10°C) introduce *Encarsia formosa* (parasitic wasp) at first sign of infestation |

# Practical preventative measures

Many simple mechanical methods can be used to exclude pests and reduce their numbers. These cause little harm to the environment, and many can be made from recycled materials.

Hand-picking is effective against many pests. Japanese beetle or cabbage caterpillars, for example, can be dealt with in this way, and many minor infestations can be squeezed with finger and thumb. Slugs and snails come out on warm, wet evenings, and they tend to return to the same site, so they can be spotted with a flashlight and picked off. Battery-operated vacuum cleaners are excellent for rounding up flying insects, such as whiteflies or flea beetles, which jump when disturbed. Use the jet from a garden hose to knock aphids and other pests off plants; some may return but many will not. This works well in combination with sticky bands (see page 36).

> Use the jet from a garden hose to knock aphids and other pests off plants

### Nets

Nets are the best way of protecting fruit. A complete cage is best and makes economic sense, but any pieces of net can be used to protect a branch or two and can be held in place with clothespins. The netting bags that fruit and nuts come in are good for individual fruits and bunches, and the feet of nylon stockings and tights do as well. Whole stockings or tights can be pulled over long branches of fruit such as redcurrants. Fine mesh bags can exclude wasps as well as birds, but may encourage mold or botrytis.

Fine netting, floating row cover, and punctured plastic sheets can be used to keep pests off vegetables and fruit and are effective at preventing carrot rust fly attacks. This fly, about the size of a housefly, has to lay its eggs next to the seedling, so a barrier gives 100 percent control. The same materials can also be used to protect cabbages from root flies and butterfly caterpillars, and to keep birds off beet and salad greens. Carrot rust flies can be stopped by a simple barrier or netting. Anything 2–3ft. (60–90cm) high around small beds stops the fly, which will go round rather than over.

### Carpet squares

Cabbage root flies need to lay their eggs in the soil next to the stem. A barrier made of 5in. (13cm) squares of thick material such as carpet underlay or cardboard fitting snugly around the stem will seal the soil underneath and prevent access.

Carpet underlay can be used to seal larger areas, trapping insect pests underneath when they emerge from hibernation or their pupae. This can considerably reduce infestations of raspberry beetles and pear midges. Carpet laid on a wet lawn will bring soil weevils and other soil pests to the surface overnight. They can be swept up or left to the birds in the morning.

*Top: A square of cardboard or carpet underlay is an effective barrier against cabbage root flies.*

*Above: Cut a slot in each piece of cardboard and fit one around the stem of each plant.*

## Bands

Bands made of cloth, carpet, and corrugated cardboard tied around trunks and stems simulate shredded bark and attract many insects. Examine your catch: beneficial ladybeetles can be retained and released to continue their good work in the garden, while the unwelcome pests are evicted.

## Earwig traps

Many creatures, especially earwigs, will crawl into hollow bamboo tubes and can then be blown out into a bucket. Earwigs are especially attracted to straw-filled flowerpots on sticks.

## Sticky traps

These are especially good in the greenhouse, where they trap many pests, especially whiteflies and thrips. Different colors attract different insects: white attracts sawflies; blue attracts thrips; and yellow attracts whiteflies. They are even more effective if they are given a pheromone scent. Hung in the trees, these sticky traps are a good way of reducing codling moth and plum fruit moth attacks.

> Earwigs are attracted to straw-filled flowerpots on sticks

## Wasp traps

Wasps are beneficial in the early season as they hunt other insects in great numbers, but in late summer they turn their attention to fruit and should be trapped. A bottle half-full of water and jelly should be given a foil cap pierced with a small hole that allows the wasps to crawl in but not to fly out. Do not use traps near flowers or with honey, because bees may also be lured in.

> Carpet underlay laid on a wet lawn will bring soil weevils and other soil pests to the surface overnight

### Slug traps

Slugs can be stopped in their tracks by barriers of wood ash, pine needles, sharp grit, or sawdust. They are also reluctant to climb over rings 4–5in. (10–13cm) high cut from plastic soda bottles and set into the ground.

Slugs can be trapped in slug "pubs," saucers, or yogurt pots half-full of fermenting beer, in which they obligingly drown themselves. Sink the pots or saucers up to their rims in the soil. Friendly ground beetles, however, also drown unless you give them some twigs to climb out on. Slugs and snails also collect under melon or orange shells and upturned saucers.

### Lures

It is possible to make lures for many pests. Tins or yogurt cartons buried in the ground with bits of potato or carrot in the base will attract mostly millipedes and sow bugs; slugs and snails will come to fruit, and wireworms will come to bran or germinating grain. Dead-fall traps follow the same principal but without the lure of fruit or vegetables to entice pests.

### Sticky bands

The bands stop pests climbing up tree trunks, which few predators need to do. They are especially effective against the female winter moth (which cannot fly), earwigs, and ants. Ants farm aphids, moving them to tender shoots and milking them for honeydew. A sticky band reduces aphid populations because the ants cannot tend and protect them. Sticky bands can be applied to the bark of old trees, but on young bark they are better used on top of a foil strip as the sticky material may soak in.

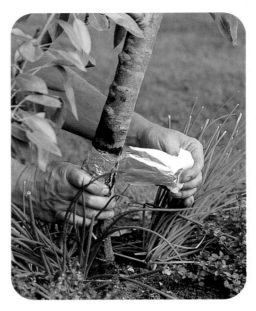

*Step 1: To apply sticky bands, first wrap a strip of foil around the trunk of the tree.*

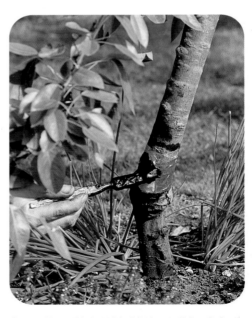

*Step 2: Next add the sticky band material, painting it on top of the foil in an even layer.*

*Step 3: Wrap a band of corrugated cardboard securely around the trunk.*

*Step 4: Tie the cardboard in place. Any beneficial insects can be simply shaken free.*

### Isolation trenches

Digging a trench about 10 x 10in. (25 x 25cm) around vegetable beds presents mice, slugs, and other small creatures with an effective barrier.

### Bird scarers

These psychological barriers work for a short time, so use several and change them daily. Scarecrows, glitterbangs (coffee packaging bags are good), unwanted CDs, and flashing humming tape (video or cassette is cheaper than the bought tapes) are worth trying. Black cotton, fur-hat cats, garden hose snakes, and paper hawks worry them, but not for very long.

### Copper tape

A hoop of copper tape around a pot will deter slugs and snails as they do not like to cross it.

### Non-set glue

Non-set glue can help to protect plants from vine weevils both indoors and out.

## Child and people proofing

Human pests can be the worst of all and their senseless damage is sometimes worse than their thefts. Fences, barriers, and locks are sadly now required, especially for succulent fruit. Signs saying "Beware of the wasps' nests!" can be more effective than "Keep out." Dogs are considered the best guards, but geese are as good and have other benefits.

# Know your worst enemies:
## directory of most common pests

### Aphids (1)

Insects (greenflies or blackflies and sometimes other colors) which live in fast-growing colonies and feed on plants' sap, weakening them and distorting growth. They also transmit viral diseases.

• Spray with soft soap or insecticidal soap.

• Pick off infected leaves and prune out infested shoots.

• Encourage natural predators, especially flower flies.

### Apple sawflies (2)

Cocoons in soil hatch out in spring. Adult flies lay eggs in open blossom. Larvae tunnel into fruitlets, feeding on flesh and seeds. Affected fruitlets drop early; mature fruit has characteristic ribbon scarring.

• Pick up and destroy infected fruitlets as soon as you notice scarring.

### Asparagus beetles (3)

Beetles and their larvae feed on foliage and stems from late spring on. Persistent attacks may check growth.

• In fall clear away plant debris, which is where beetles overwinter.

### Big bud mites (4)

Mites breed inside developing buds of blackcurrants, causing them to become round and swollen. Mites carry reversion disease (see page 48), which causes slow deterioration of bush and poor cropping.

• Remove and burn all swollen buds before spring.

• In severe cases cut back all growth to ground level and discard cuttings.

5 Blackflies

2 Apple sawflies

4 Big bud mites

1 Aphids

3 Asparagus beetles

## Blackflies (5)

These aphids cluster on growing tips of fava beans in late spring and can spread to rest of plant, stunting growth and reducing crop. May spread to other beans, beet, chard, and ornamentals.

- Sow hardy varieties in fall so that plants are tougher and less attractive in spring.
- Pinch out affected tips.
- Spray with soft soap.

## Cabbage root flies (6)

Larvae eat roots, causing stunted, wilting plants. They overwinter as shiny brown cocoons in soil and emerge to lay eggs around plants.

- Grow plants under netting or floating row cover or lay 5in. (13cm) square mats of carpet underlay around plants so they fit snugly around stems.
- Intercrop with beans in alternate rows to confuse pest.
- Dig over soil in winter after infected crop.

7 Cabbage white caterpillars

## Cabbage white caterpillars (7)

Large, plump caterpillars feed on leaves and bore into the hearts of cabbages and lettuces.

- Pick off the caterpillars by hand.
- Grow plants under fine netting or floating row cover to stop butterflies laying eggs on leaves.
- Spray with *Bacillus thuringiensis* (bacterium), which kills caterpillars but is harmless to humans.

## Carrot rust flies (8)

Larvae feed on roots of carrot and other root vegetables. Seedlings may be killed; older plants will be stunted. Roots are tunneled through with white larvae inside. Flies overwinter in soil and in roots left in ground.

- Sow in early spring or midsummer.
- Grow carrots under fine netting or floating row cover or erect a barrier of fine netting about 30in. (75cm) high around bed.
- Lift and destroy infested plants immediately.

## Codling moths (9)

Affect mainly apples, pears, and quinces. Adults hatch from cocoons in midsummer to lay eggs in leaves or fruit. Caterpillars tunnel into maturing fruit and feed for several weeks before pupating.

- Hang pheromone traps, containing a sticky substance that attracts male moths, in trees.

8 Carrot rust flies

6 Cabbage root flies

9 Codling moths

## Cutworms (10)

Moth caterpillars live in the soil and feed at night on the soil's surface, eating young plants at soil level and attacking stems and roots of vegetables and strawberries.
- Protect individual plants with collars.
- Hoe and dig regularly in winter to expose them to birds.
- Pick them off by hand at night.

## Earwigs (11)

Earwigs attack fruit trees (especially apples) and flowers. They do eat codling moth eggs and woolly aphids, so should be left if possible.
- If a problem trap them in flowerpots filled with straw and supported upside down on canes.

## Flea beetles (12)

Attacks cabbages and other brassicas, covering leaves with small holes. The beetles hibernate in plant debris and under loose tree bark.
- Cover plants with fine netting or floating row cover.
- Go along rows with sticky greased board because beetles jump up when disturbed.
- Spray with pyrethrum.

## Leatherjackets (13)

The larvae of craneflies live in the soil and are mainly a problem on vegetable gardens dug from old lawns or old pasture land or on very weedy soil. They feed on vegetable roots (especially those of brassicas).
- Keep soil weed-free.
- Hoe and dig the soil regularly to expose them to the birds.

## Mealybugs (14)

Cacti, succulents, and many other plants, especially under glass, are often affected. Pinkish gray, soft-bodied insects suck sap from young stems. In heavy infestation foliage and fruit are sticky with honeydew, on which black sooty mold develops.
- Spray with pyrethrum.
- Under glass introduce *Cryptolaemus montrouzieri* (predatory ladybeetle).

11 Earwigs

13 Leatherjackets

10 Cutworms

12
Flea beetles

14 Mealybugs

## Onion flies (15)

Resembling small houseflies, these attack onions, leeks, and shallots. Eggs are laid near the base of seedlings, and maggots bore into young bulbs, causing leaves to turn yellow. Remove infected plants to limit spread.

• Dig over infected land in winter to destroy the larvae.

• Grow seedlings under fine netting or floating row cover.

## Pea moths (16)

Caterpillars live and feed inside pea pods. Moth lays eggs in midsummer on flowering pea plants. Caterpillars eat their way into developing pods.

• Sow peas early and late to avoid midsummer flowering time.

• Dig over infested soil in winter to disturb pupating caterpillars.

• Protect plants in flower with fine netting or floating row cover.

16 Pea moths

15 Onion flies

17
Pear midges

## Pear midges (17)

Females lay eggs in unopened flower buds. Larvae hatch out within developing fruitlets. After petal fall fruitlets turn black and drop. Maggots then crawl into soil to pupate.

• Collect and compost all fallen fruitlets.

• Remove affected fruitlets as soon as noticed.

• Dig over soil near affected trees in winter to expose cocoons to birds.

## Pea weevils (18)

Also affects beans, chewing a scalloped edge on leaves. Not a serious problem on strong plants, but young plants may die back. The weevils overwinter in plant debris and larvae emerge as adults in midsummer.

• Encourage strong, fast growth.

• Sow beans under cover and plant out when growing strongly.

## Raspberry beetles (19)

Adults feed on raspberry blossom in late spring. Larvae tunnel into ripening fruit and may not be noticed until fruit is picked. Pupae overwinter in soil near canes.

• Lightly hoe soil in fall and winter to expose pupae to birds.

19 Raspberry beetles

18 Pea weevils

### Red spider mites (20)

Usually a greenhouse pest but can attack strawberries, raspberries, and currants in hot weather. The undersurfaces of leaves become bronzed; older leaves are withered or crisp. Greenish mites are visible with magnification.

• Cut off all leaves after harvesting fruit.
• Use *Phytoseiulus persimilis* (predatory mite) in greenhouses.

### Scale insects (21)

Small, flat insects attach themselves to fruit and other trees, vines, and ornamental plants under glass. They suck sap and smear leaves with honeydew, which encourages sooty mold.

• Spray with insecticidal soap.
• Use *Metaphycus helvolus* (predatory wasp).

### Stem nematodes (22)

Attack a wide range of fruit, vegetables, and ornamental plants. Onion and leek leaves swell and distort, and bulbs crack and rot. Nematodes survive in the soil for a considerable time. There is no cure for infected plants.

• Discard all infected plants.
• Grow only brassicas and lettuces on infested soil for two years.
• Keep area weed free.

### Vine weevils (23)

Beetles feed on leaf margins of many plants, especially rhododendrons, euonymus, and hydrangeas. Plump white maggots attack roots, especially of container-grown plants, and tubers of ornamental plants under glass. The roots are usually destroyed and plants will not recover.

• Use *Heterorhabditis megidis* or *Steinernema carpocapsae* (pathogenic nematodes) applied in late summer.

20 Red spider mites

21 Scale insects

22 Stem nematodes

23 Vine weevils

## Wasps (24)

A pest only in high summer and early fall, when fruit is damaged, and especially in hot, dry weather, when numbers increase.

• Suspend wasp traps in trees.

## Whiteflies (25)

Small, winged insects, which live on leaves of brassicas and fly up in clouds when disturbed. Young scales remain on the plants.

• Dig up winter brassicas as soon as cropping is finished and bury in trench or compost pile before planting out new ones.
• Remove leaves with visible scales before they turn into adults.
• Suck up adults with mini-vacuum cleaner.
• Spray with insecticidal soap.
• Under glass use *Encarsia formosa* (parasitic wasp) at first sign of infestation.

## Wireworms (26)

Larvae of the click beetle, which lays eggs in grass or weedy soil. Attack stems and tubers of many vegetables (including onions, potatoes, carrots, peas, and beans). More of a problem on old pasture land.

• Keep land cultivated to expose them to birds.
• Catch them on small pieces of carrot or potato spiked on sticks and buried and renewed regularly.

## Woolly aphids (27)

A species that attacks tree trunks, branches, and twigs. Aphid covers itself with white, woollike covering. Attacked wood becomes swollen and may crack, allowing entry to canker and other diseases; soft, lumpy galls appear on bark.

• Spray with soft soap or insecticidal soap.
• If this does not work, cut out infestation.

25 Whiteflies

26 Wireworms

27 Woolly aphids

24 Wasps

# Know your worst enemies:
## directory of most common diseases

### American gooseberry mildew (1)

Also affects blackcurrants. Powdery, white coating on leaves, shoots, and fruits; patches become brown and felted.

- Avoid overcrowded bushes and weedy soil.
- Prune regularly to keep bushes open and to admit light and air.
- Cut out and discard diseased shoots.
- Spray with Bordeaux mixture at flower stage.

### Apple canker (2)

Destructive disease (also of plums and pears), causing sunken, discolored patches on bark; branches become swollen. White pustules appear in summer and small, red fruiting bodies appear in winter.

- Cut out and discard diseased patches, branches, or shoots, cutting back to clean wood.
- Feed and mulch to encourage vigor.

### Bacterial canker (3)

A serious disease of plums, with bacteria living in the leaves. Elongated cankers on branches exude gum; leaves have brown, circular spots; buds fail to open on cankered branches; if leaves develop, they yellow and drop as branch dies back.

- Cut out and discard affected wood.
- Spray with Bordeaux mixture in midsummer and again in early and midfall.

3 Bacterial canker

1 American gooseberry mildew

2 Apple canker

## Blackleg (4)

A bacterial disease of potatoes, causing foliage to turn yellow and stems to blacken and die. Tubers may also be affected, developing a brown, slimy rot inside.

- Remove and discard affected plants.
- Lift the rest of the crop to avoid contact with infected tubers.
- Do not save any tubers for seed.
- Buy only certified seed to avoid blackleg.

## Botrytis (5)

A common greenhouse problem of grapes, strawberries, cucumbers, tomatoes, and lettuces. Affected plants are covered with a velvety, gray-brown fungus, which thrives in cold, damp conditions.

- Remove dead leaves and overripe fruit.
- Ventilate to reduce humidity.
- Water in the morning, not at night.
- Do not overwater.
- Use fertilizers sparingly.

## Clubroot (6)

Disease (mainly of brassicas) causing wilting, stunted plants. When pulled up, roots are swollen and distorted. Clubroot prefers acidic conditions and can stay in the ground for 20 years.

- Dig up and discard affected plants.
- Practice good crop rotation and never grow brassicas in infected soil.
- Keep ground well limed.
- Raise seedlings in pots to get them off to a good start.
- Never buy in seedlings.

> Clubroot prefers acidic conditions and can stay in the ground for 20 years

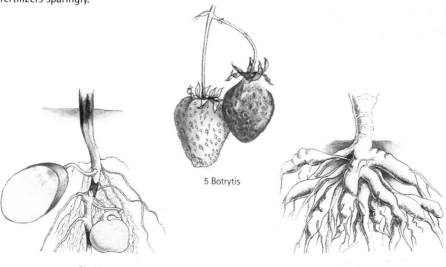

5 Botrytis

4 Blackleg

6 Clubroot

## Cucumber mosaic virus (7)

Affects cucurbits (especially marrows) and is spread by aphids. Diseased plants are stunted and have puckered, distorted leaves with yellow mottling on them.
• Destroy infected plants immediately.
• Encourage aphid predators by planting marigolds and nasturtiums in the vegetable garden.

## Damping off (8)

A fungal disease that causes seedlings to collapse at ground level. Troublesome where seedlings are overcrowded or growing in wet, compacted soil.
• Sow seeds thinly and use sterilized soil or potting mix with a fine texture.
• Avoid overwatering.
• Use clean municipal water (not from a well or barrel, which may contain infective organisms).

## Fireblight (9)

Bacterial disease affecting various trees and shrubs. Cankers appear at base of dead shoots and red-brown discoloration appears inside. Causes dieback or browning of leaves.
• Cut out diseased wood 2ft. (60cm) below affected tissue.
• Disinfect pruning tools after use.

## Leaf spot (10)

Many plants affected, especially in wet seasons. Leaf surface can become completely brown and shriveled; plant loses vigor.
• Remove and discard diseased leaves.
• Spray plants with Bordeaux mixture.
• If brassicas are affected, remove alternate plants to improve ventilation.
• Do not overuse nitrogen-rich fertilizer.

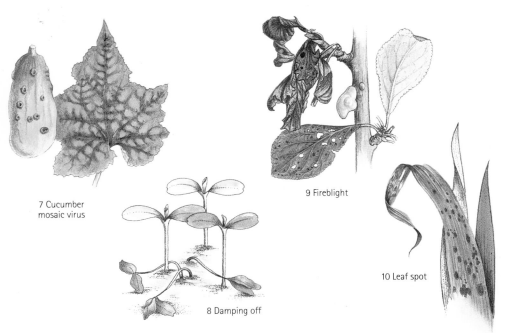

7 Cucumber mosaic virus

9 Fireblight

8 Damping off

10 Leaf spot

## Mildew (11)

Downy and powdery mildews are seen as pale gray fungus on leaves, flowers, and young shoots. Affects many ornamentals, including roses. Downy mildew affects vines and vegetables.

- Remove and discard affected leaves.
- Spray with Bordeaux mixture.
- Avoid overcrowding and humid conditions.

## Peach leaf curl (12)

Leaves become thickened and curl; red blisters develop and are covered with fungal spores. Leaves fall early, and tree is weakened. Fungus overwinters in bark or on shoots. The spores are carried by rain.

- Spray with Bordeaux mixture in late winter or early spring (repeating 10–14 days later) to prevent spores from entering buds.
- Spray again just before leaf fall.
- Spread out floating row cover over espalier and fan-trained trees to keep off rain.

## Potato blight (13)

Causes brown patches on leaves, especially in warm, wet weather; foliage blackens and dies; tubers may rot. Spreads rapidly in humid conditions.

- Spray with Bordeaux mixture every two weeks until harvesting.
- In severe cases, cut down and discard foliage.
- Delay harvesting for two or three weeks so tubers are not affected.
- Grow resistant cultivars such as 'Cara', 'Wilja', and 'Kondor'.

12 Peach leaf curl

11 Mildew

13 Potato blight

## Reversion disease (14)

Carried by big bud mites (see page 38), which attack blackcurrants. Difficult to recognize, but leaves are narrower than usual and have fewer than five pairs of veins on the main lobe. Flower buds turn bright magenta (instead of gray), bushes lose vigor, and crop is reduced. There is no known cure.

- Dig up and discard affected plants.
- Plant certified disease-free stock on a different site.

## Rose black spot (15)

Common fungal disease, especially in wet, humid weather. Leaf spots may merge into large, dead areas; leaves wither and die.

- Prune hard in fall and discard prunings to kill off overwintering spores.
- Pick up and discard fallen leaves in fall.
- Mulch soil well.
- Plant roses in a sunny, open site and space well to ensure good ventilation.

## Rust (16)

Affects a wide range of plants. Leaves and stems develop red, brown, or yellow pustules. Leaves may wither and die. Whole plant may wilt.

- Remove and discard affected leaves and whole plant if severely affected.
- Spray plants with sulfur.
- Under glass improve ventilation to reduce humidity and make sure water droplets do not remain on leaves.

> Plant roses in a sunny, open site and space well to ensure good ventilation

15 Rose black spot

14 Reversion disease

16 Rust

## Scab (17)

Disease affecting potatoes and causing ugly, ragged scabs on the skin. Most often found in dry, sandy soil lacking organic matter.
• Dig in plenty of humus (compost or manure) and do not lime soil before planting.
• Water in dry weather.
• Add a layer of grass clippings to the trench at planting.
• Grow resistant cultivars such as 'Arran Pilot', 'Arran Comet', 'King Edward, or 'Maris Peer'.

## Silverleaf (18)

A fungal disease of fruit trees, caused when spores enter through wounds. Leaves become silvered and then brown; progressive dieback affects branches; small, purple, white, or brown fruiting bodies develop on dead wood.
• Cut back all dead branches at least 6in. (15cm) beyond infection in summer (when there is least chance of new infection).
• Sterilize pruning tools before and after use.

## Soft rot (19)

Affects rutabagas and turnips, particularly in wet weather. Flesh rots into a foul-smelling mess while rind remains intact. Most troublesome on heavily manured and badly drained soil.
• Practice crop rotation.
• Make sure drainage is good and grow on deep beds to improve drainage.
• Control slugs to save foliage because disease can enter through wounds.
• Remove and discard affected plants.

> Sterilize pruning tools before and after use to avoid silverleaf

17 Scab

18 Silverleaf

19 Soft rot

# Weeds in the organic garden

Any piece of ground left untended rapidly becomes covered with weeds. As the weeds slowly build up the fertility of the soil, the patch of ground becomes suitable for nettles and tree seedlings. A profusion of these weeds, especially nettles, can indicate a potentially rich site. Deep-rooted weeds like dock and thistle are also good for the soil as they bring up nutrients, making them available for future crops.

The types of weed will always be those most suited to the conditions, so:

• If they consist of acidic-loving plants such as daisies, small nettles, and sorrels, the topsoil is probably acidic.

• Lime soils are indicated by cowslips, knapweed, and silverweed.

• Damp conditions encourage nettles, buttercups, bugle, and rushes.

• Lots of docks means that horses or their manure have been on the land as the seeds pass through their intestines unchecked.

• Lots of tomato seedlings could mean that sewage sludge has been used.

• Beware of any land that grows few weeds!

## Good weeds and bad weeds

Weeds are, as we are always being told, just plants in the wrong place. Many are otherwise valuable garden plants or even crops—poppies, feverfew, and red valerian, for example. Many weeds are edible: chickweed and dandelion leaves are delicious in salads, lamb's quarters, nettles, and bishop's weed can be cooked like spinach, while the roots of dandelion, horseradish, and vetch are all edible. In some gardens, weeds may be the last remnants of the original flora and so help preserve insect and wildlife populations. A stand of weeds not only fixes and stabilizes the soil, but can also act as a miniature hedge and windbreak, sheltering emerging seedlings, although it should be eradicated before it competes too much.

Remember, too, before you get rid of all weeds that some are attractive to bees, butterflies, and insects. They should not be allowed to compete with other plants, of course, but if you have a patch of ground at the end of the garden where they will do no harm, it is worth allowing some to survive. Weeds that attract beneficial insects include nettles, poppies, groundsel, robert geranium, and dandelion.

Most of all, weeds are a useful source of fertility, admirably suited to their conditions by self-selection. They produce a wealth of green manure at times when other plants cannot use the soil and act as valuable groundcover over winter. They are also superb mineral accumulators, making these accessible to crops after they have been dug in or mulched. Clovers and vetches fix nitrogen, comfrey is well known for accumulating potassium, as are nettles and thistles, while phosphorus is collected by lamb's quarters, sorrel, yarrow, and jimsonweed. Stubborn-rooted perennials, such as comfrey and nettles, will have to be mulched rather than dug in if they are used as green manure—and you will need to dig up the roots later, unless you want an annual crop.

# Weed control in non-soil areas

Walkways, driveways, decks, and patios are often a problem because windblown seeds lodge in every niche. Prevention is better than cure, so either point up holes and cracks with cement or mastic (after cleaning them all out by hand with a knife and a pressure hose) or grow plants you want there. Working in a mixture of potting soil and thyme and chamomile seeds will prevent other plants getting in. Flame-guns (see page 53) are best where they can safely be used, knives remove weeds from cracks;

> Weeds are just plants in the wrong place

I use a weed whacker to flay them, although the occasional stone has done for a window or two. A carpet or plastic sheet laid on top for a few weeks will kill off many weeds. It can also be laid permanently and covered with fresh gravel.

# Groundcover plants

Mulching (see pages 54–7) under shrubs and over large areas becomes expensive in materials and time as there will always be some weeds that arrive on the wind. It then becomes more effective to use groundcover plants, especially grass which is so simply maintained. Other alternatives include:

• **Ivy** in shady areas; it is easily removed with a weed whacker.

• Planting out bulbs, primroses, violets, and other naturalizing plants can further improve appearances and the wildlife habitat without upsetting weed control: a weed whacker can be used up to and around the chosen plants.

• **Mints** are the most vigorous and beneficial groundcover plants wherever height allows; these suppress most weeds and are loved by insects when they flower. They can be kept within bounds by a mown grass path.

*Above: Primroses can be naturalized, with or without a carpet of ivy around them, to form groundcover.*

*Below: Mints make very effective groundcover and their flowers will attract beneficial insects.*

# Controlling weeds

After grass cutting, weeding probably takes up most gardening time. Weeds will rapidly choke plants and spoil the garden, lock up fertility in seeds and roots, and harbor pests and diseases.

Organic gardeners do not use chemical herbicides, which kill not only weeds but other forms of life as well. As with pests, the aim is control, not elimination, as some weeds have their uses as well as drawbacks.

There are many ways to kill weeds. Some, like digging up, are better used to break new ground, while others, like hoeing, can be used to maintain control. Mulching is probably most important, as it not only prevents weed seeds germinating but also conserves the fertility and moisture of the soil.

## Hygiene

Take precautions to prevent weeds being brought into your garden—dirty manures, uncomposted mulches, and bought-in plants smuggle in seeds.
• Protect flowerbeds, gravel paths and driveways by never letting anything set seed nearby or upwind.
• Rotation is as useful. By moving the crop and changing the conditions no weed species is favored and allowed to become established.

## Digging

If you are starting a new border where the ground has been under grass for a while, digging is the best method. Regular grass cutting will have reduced weed populations, leaving grasses and rosette weeds such as daisies. From early fall to late winter the turfgrass can be skimmed off and stacked for loam, used elsewhere, or dug in. Tap-rooted weeds can be dug up as they are uncovered and wilted for compost. Removing creeping weeds, such as quackgrass, is exceedingly laborious; completely excluding light with a black plastic mulch is easier.
• Dig in overwintering groundcover weeds in the early spring, so that they have time to decay before anything is planted.
• Dig and chop small areas methodically rather than labor with larger pieces.

## Rototilling

Rototilling kills earthworms, damages some soil textures, and is noisy, dangerous work. It is not really suitable for ground that is badly infested with perennial weeds as most rototillers have insufficient power, and if they succeed they chop roots into many pieces which then regrow. However, they are useful for incorporating green manures and overwintered annual weeds. They are most definitely not for the smaller garden because of their awkwardness in confined spaces. To break in a large garden, which is not compacted and is down to clean turfgrass or light cover, rototill two or three times in spring, about two weeks apart, to incorporate the cover as well as any regrowth as it occurs.

- Alternatively, lift and invert the surface layer of soil in shallow slices, and hoe after a week or two to prevent the weeds from re-rooting.

## Handweeding

Handweeding is the best way to remove weeds from among plants. Kneeling pads protect the knees, and a sharp knife helps cut stubborn roots rather than pulling them up with a lot of soil. Remove the weeds close to the plants first, then the larger ones between. Small seedling weeds may then be killed with the edge of the knife or a hand rake rather than by pulling them up.

Although it is laborious, you can convert perennial weeds into fertility if the new leaves are pulled off each week until the root system expires. Some much-feared weeds, such as bishop's weed, can be eliminated in a season if all leaves and shoots are removed weekly.

## Hoeing

Severing the top growth just below ground level is most effective, but the hoe must be sharp. In heavy, sticky, or stony ground it may pay to put a hoeing mulch of builder's sand or sifted compost on top of the soil to make the going easier.

Hoeing is good for keeping borders clear. Annual weeds need hoeing every two weeks from early spring to late summer, but little thereafter. Hoeing every two weeks takes little time, but if left longer the weeds become established and take more effort. Hoeing is effective against perennial weeds if done weekly, so the top growth is continually hoed off. The roots become exhausted using up their reserves to make new growth, and will die.

## Flame-gunning

This is not as frightening as it sounds. A gas or paraffin blowtorch is passed over the weeds to cook but not char the leaves, leaving them to weaken the root system as they wither. It is effective against seedlings, but if the weeds are established some may recover and need a second treatment. It is possible to kill perennial weeds with repeated weekly flame-gunning, though it is more ecological to dig them up and compost them.

Timing a flame-gunning just before a crop emerges can be useful; it removes the weeds without disturbing the crop or bringing up more weed seeds. For example, carrots take 12–18 days to germinate so all weeds emerging in the first 10 days can be removed with a treatment on day 11. The carrots then emerge, deterring further weeds.

## Can I use a flame-gun?

| |
| --- |
| ✓ For large areas: Yes, it's most useful for this |
| ✓ Seedbeds: Yes |
| ✓ Gravel driveways: Yes, but keep away from cars, buildings, and inflammable materials |
| ✓ Trees: Yes, just up to large trees' trunks |
| ✓ Brussels sprouts: Yes, if mature |
| ✓ Herbaceous plants: Yes, while dormant if the crown is covered with sand |
| ✓ Rock gardens: Yes, use a small blowtorch |
| ✓ Pathways and patios: Yes, use a small blowtorch, hot-air paint stripper, boiling water, or even a steam iron |
| ✗ Conifers: No |
| ✗ Evergreens: No |
| ✗ Hedges: No |
| ✗ Plants with dead leaves: No |

# Mulching

Mulching is probably the most important yet underused method of weed control. Mulching materials can be expensive to buy, but can save much time and effort by suppressing weeds. They will all help moisture conservation, and they encourage growth by helping to maintain a stable soil temperature. Organic mulches, when they are applied regularly, add fertility and also amend the texture of the soil.

All mulches can be applied at any time but are most beneficial if they are applied in spring, when the soil is warming up but before winter rain has evaporated. Mulches which are applied too early will keep the soil cold and slow down growth. If there is a long period of dry weather it is a good idea to rake or roll aside mulches when it rains and replace them afterwards, to prevent the mulch soaking up all the water and stopping it reaching the soil.

> Mulches are the easiest way of breaking in new ground

## Advantages

Mulches are the easiest way of breaking in new ground, as well as a good way of keeping weeds down later. Providing the top growth is not woody and has at least been cut with a rotary mower, an area can be turned into weed-free, clean soil in six months with little effort or preparation.

• All weeds are killed by completely excluding light with impenetrable mulches.

• Tougher perennial weeds are stopped only by thick, opaque plastic or fabric, such as old carpet, but most weeds can be killed off with a thick mulch of straw, hay, or grass clippings on top of cardboard and newspaper.

• Avoid using opaque black plastic on areas larger than 3ft. (1m) because lack of air and moisture can cause problems with the soil; on these large areas it is better to use perforated black plastic or old carpet.

• It helps if an isolation trench 12in. (30cm) deep and wide is dug round the perimeter first and the mulch continued over the edge.

Mulching new ground works best if an impenetrable mulch is put down just as the weeds have started into growth, flattening them underneath—usually in early spring when the soil is also full of water; doing this after midspring is far less effective. The weeds turn yellow through lack of light and rapidly rot, followed by their root systems, feeding soil life and increasing fertility. After a month or so the sheet of mulch can be rolled back early in the morning to expose any creatures for the birds. Worms and beneficial insects move quickly and escape, but pests, such as slugs, are slower and do not.

If an area is mulched like this in early spring, it can then be cropped from late spring. The weeds may recover if the mulch is simply removed, but some vegetables can be planted out through holes in the mulch, where they will grow wonderfully in the moist, enriched soil underneath. Tomatoes, zucchini, squashes, cucumbers, melons, and corn will all do very well.

Top: A carpet mulch gets to work breaking up new ground. This is the result after 10 days.

Middle: This is the result after three weeks. Most of the weeds have now disappeared.

Bottom: After several months the weeds have rotted down and been incorporated into the soil.

necessary. Almost all the weeds and roots will have rotted and disappeared, leaving a rich texture and natural stratification that may be better left undisturbed. Winter crops can be planted through the mulch, or the soil can be overwintered under a green manure, which has the advantage of restoring the pH of the soil (which tends to drop under mulches).

In the same way, green manures and overwintered weeds can be mulched in early spring with sheets of plastic or fabric or even under large quantities of grass clippings. Again, crops can then be planted through the mulch into the enriched soil in late spring. Compost can be added as well before mulching for optimum results when growing hungry feeders.

Impenetrable or loose mulches can be applied onto bare soil or annual weeds in the vegetable garden in the fall months.

• They protect the soil from erosion and encourage soil life, especially earthworms, so that when the mulch is removed or planted through in spring the soil will have excellent texture and very good fertility.

• Fall mulching can benefit herbaceous and less hardy plants by protecting them from frost, although plants subject to rot in damp conditions should be mulched only with light, airy materials, such as loose straw.

Brassicas also thrive, but most of these plants occupy the land through winter so do not fit in if the area is needed for fall.

In fall after any crop has been removed, the mulch can be removed and the area dug over if

*Above: Composted or chipped bark makes an attractive mulch for a path.*

## Disadvantages

Mulches do have a few drawbacks other than the cost, however.

- Sheet mulches may encourage pests underneath, such as voles, moles, and slugs, and loose ones tend to be scattered onto lawns by birds.
- There is also a danger of rotting crowns or bark in excessively damp conditions, and grafts may take root if the union is covered by a mulch.
- Mulches can also seal in the soil warmth, and growth above becomes more prone to frost than it would over bare soil.

## Plastic mulches

Plastic sheets are a great aid to weed control, but they are unsightly, costly, and environmentally undesirable. Nevertheless, they have a number of uses in the organic garden. Clear plastic, similar to that used for hoop houses, can be pinned to the ground to warm up the soil in spring and encourage flushes of weeds. Black or opaque plastic sheet, thick enough to exclude all light, warms the soil and kills weeds, even perennials. It can be laid permanently and then covered with a loose mulch of wood chippings to improve the appearance so that it is suitable for shrub gardens, soft fruit, and other permanent plantings. In the same way it can be laid under gravel paths and driveways. Use perforated plastic on large areas to prevent water problems and lack of aeration to the soil. Black-and-white plastic sheets are useful: after the black surface has warmed the soil and killed weeds it can be reversed to the white side to reflect light onto the plants and confuse pests.

- Squares of plastic, with a slit for access and the edges buried in soil, make a superb mulch for young trees, keeping them weed free and preventing evaporation for a year or two.
- Long strips 3ft. (1m) or so wide are excellent for starting hedges; cuttings of easy rooters can even be pushed through them.
- Strips of plastic can also be used for strawberries, vegetables, and particularly lettuces, which then get less dirty, though slugs may become more of a problem.

All plastic sheets have to be well anchored with earth or stones, otherwise in high winds there is a danger of them and the plants blowing away or becoming damaged.

# Types of mulch

| Material | Type | Advantages | Disadvantages |
|---|---|---|---|
| Cocoa shells | Loose | • High in nitrogen • Very good at deterring slugs | • Should be laid to a depth of about 2in. (5cm) to be effective • Light and easily blown initially |
| Composted bark | Loose | • Attractive | • Scattered by birds • Expensive for large areas • Should be laid to a depth of about 3in. (8cm) to be effective |
| Builder's sand and Gravel | Loose | • Attractive • Suitable for plants that like Mediterranean-type conditions | • Will not amend soil fertility |
| Leafmold | Loose | • Home-made • Use over a sheet mulch | • Better used in potting mixes |
| Paper and cardboard | Sheet | • Readily available and free • Useful for keeping salad greens clean in the greenhouse • Good for keeping down weed growth when used under another material • Used under loose material will prevent birds mixing weed seeds into the mulch | • Too light in open garden unless used with another mulch or weights on top • Rots rapidly |
| Plastic sheets | Sheet | • Cheap • Efficient | • Unattractive • Expensive • Environmentally undesirable • Prevents soil aeration |
| Semi-permeable membrane | Sheet | • Resistant to weed growth • Porosity allows better soil aeration and less water run-off than plastic • Ideal for valuable crops (e.g. strawberries) | • Expensive over large areas • Environmentally dubious |
| Prunings (woody) | Loose | • Free | • Must be composted before use |
| Straw and hay | Loose | • Good soil amendment | • May include its own seeds |
| Wood chips | Loose | • Good semi-formal path | • Must be composted for other uses |

# What weed is that?

There are two types of weed, perennials and annuals, and once the former have been totally eliminated the latter are easy to control with a little time and effort.

## Annual weeds

Annual weed seeds germinate as soon as soil is exposed to the light, warmth, and wet, but they can be prevented from doing so by mulching or deep burial. As seedlings, these weeds are relatively easy to kill, but they rapidly become tougher. Some can even set seed lying on the ground if they have reached the flowering stage. From the point of view of weed control it doesn't matter if the seedling weed is actually a biennial or annual; it is small and easily killed if it is not long established. These are the best weeds to use as green manure or winter groundcover, as they are not deep-rooting and are easy to eradicate.

Once all the perennial weeds have been cleared from an area there are almost certainly going to be thick flushes of weed seedlings for a year or two, but after some seasons of regular weeding there will be fewer seedlings.

If you want to use annual weeds to give good winter cover on the soil, digging or deep raking will bring up more seeds. Also, selected weeds or other favored plants can be allowed to seed in vegetable gardens and other areas needing cover and the added benefit of green manuring.

Where the weeds are being mulched, dug, or hoed in, their goodness is retained. They can also be put on the compost pile, and their fertility thus used for more important crops. All weeds can be composted, but those with pernicious roots should be withered on a path first. Alternatively rot them along with seeding weeds in a rain barrel for a few weeks and you get a free liquid feed into the bargain. Diseased weeds are probably best burned.

## Perennial weeds

Established perennial weeds survive from year to year by means of underground roots and bulbs, and the worst creep, spread, and regrow from pieces of root. Most of them also produce seeds. Weeds such as docks, horseradish, and dandelions have long taproots which store food for the plants, bringing up water and nutrients from deep in the soil. Destroying the leaves once is no good, for the root will simply produce new ones. If you cut off the root, leaving even a small piece in the soil, it will grow again, though dock can be killed by taking out the top 4in. (10cm) of root.

> Never plant up beds or borders without first removing or killing all perennial weeds

> Where the weeds are being mulched, dug, or hoed in, their goodness is retained

# Annual weeds

Shepherd's purse

Groundsel

Hairy bittercress

Annual meadow grass

Creepers such as quackgrass, nettles, and bishop's weed develop a mass of stems just below ground. These have to be dug up, with every small piece of stem removed, for again even a small section of stem left behind will develop new plants.

If you have taken over a new garden or joined a community garden, or are simply breaking in a new piece of ground, it is essential to clear each and every bit of these weeds. Clearing them methodically reduces later weed control effort to the seedling annuals, which can be easily hoed or mulched. Never plant up soil without first removing or killing all perennial weeds—if they are allowed to interpenetrate plant roots, weeding becomes far more difficult.

## Perennial weeds

Celandine

Japanese knotweed

Horseradish

Bitter dock

Buttercup

Dandelion

Heliotrope

Creeping thistle

Horsetail

Quackgrass

Bishop's weed

Stinging nettle

# Step 4 Choose the right plants

Using good methods is 95 percent of organic gardening. Plants want to grow, and will if we give them the right conditions. So choose plants that are suited to their local conditions, and avoid those that present obvious problems. There is no point in trying to grow watermelons in a temperate climate, rhododendrons on alkaline soil, or cauliflowers in hot, dry, sandy soil. Grow plants that are suited to your soil and climate and they will succeed.

# Factors to keep in mind

There are various factors to keep in mind when choosing plants. As well as the general conditions of basic soil type and climate, which will dictate the types of plants, you also need to look at aspect (how much sun the area gets, from which direction, and the amount of exposure to wind) and microclimate.

## Soil type

Both the acidity and moisture-retaining properties of your soil have a profound effect on your general gardening and the former is only easily overcome by growing in containers. You can do a little to alter the acidity of your soil but for many more plants it is better to change their root conditions. This usually means lightening heavy soils to make them warmer and freer draining to suit the dry sun-lovers, and manuring and mulching light soils to make them suited to heavy feeders and those that tolerate but dislike lime.

## Aspect

Much of the skill of gardening lies in selecting plants that will benefit most or endure well the varying conditions a small garden imposes. Most effectively have walls all round and many are tilted away from the sunniest direction. In the northern hemisphere walls facing south are warmest year-round as they get most sun, and this applies to gardens as well. However, one gardener's sunny wall is another's shady one and with small gardens many areas are shady and few sunny. In the area below each wall the conditions are very different and completely different plants will succeed in each. In sunnier south-facing gardens or beds you can obviously succeed better with the many plants that need the most sun, and fruit and vegetables will be sweeter. However, shady north-facing gardens and borders can still grow many vegetables well and some fruit, and will provide better conditions for many foliage plants, especially in a dry summer.

The need to differentiate between east and west is less obvious, but facing east can be a problem for some plants; exposure to the rising sun can be fatal to frosted blossoms. Worse still can be exposure to icy blasts from winds at inopportune times such as during fruit blossom. Facing into the prevailing winds also brings more rain and such areas are not suitable for plants that like to be warm, dry, and sheltered. In addition, it is important to think about your own enjoyment of the garden: plants that flower best in the morning or the evening should be placed where you can get the best of them for most appreciation, and a summerhouse or seat should face west because it is more likely to be used in the evening.

## Microclimate

Every garden has its own microclimate and smaller ones within it. Because of many factors, particularly the aspect of the site as a whole, the amount of shade from surroundings, the shape and nature of the walls and fences, the heat escaping from homes and drains, and the pooling of cold air down slopes creating frost pockets, each and every spot is slightly different. Although you may enjoy much the same conditions as others in your vicinity, your garden has within it spots that at different times of year and day are much more favorable to some plant or another. It is also within our power to improve these spots much further, which in temperate climates usually means increasing shelter from the wind and capturing more sun. In sunnier climes, however, providing shade is as important for many plants.

> One gardener's sunny wall is another's shady one

*Below: This mixed border shows shasta daisies, bergamot, and phlox blooming in midsummer, while trees and other perennials provide structure during the winter months.*

# Disease-resistant plants

In many ways the plants we grow have been selected because they are inherently trouble free, but few cultivars are immune to all pests and diseases. The more important crops are grown most frequently, and thus have acquired the most pests and diseases to bother them.

For these economically important crops, which include some popular ornamentals, much research has been done to find varieties resistant to the common ailments. Most success has been against diseases, especially with those of vegetable crops. Also, roses have long been bred with considerable mildew and black spot resistance.

> Pests are harder to discourage as the hungry critters want their lunch

Pests are harder to discourage as the hungry critters want their lunch. However, by changing the smell and color, the pest can sometimes be confused. Unfortunately, after a time, resistant plants start to fail as the pests and the diseases alter and start to attack again. However, for the most important crops new varieties are continually being introduced, which makes recommending any one variety pointless. Because of all the effort which is made is into securing the crop, little attention is paid to cooking and eating qualities. So a small drawback in choosing resistant varieties is that this inevitably entails some loss of flavor or quality in comparison with other varieties. Thus it is a good idea to grow at least a couple of sorts with one for reliability and another for flavor.

*Above: The 'Muscat Hamburg' vine.*

*Above: The yellow tomato variety 'Golden Sunrise'.*

# Crops with some resistance

| Crop | Diseases and pests | Crop | Diseases and pests |
|------|--------------------|------|--------------------|
| Asparagus | Botrytis | Onions | Downy mildew<br>Botrytis<br>White rot |
| Beans | Mosaic virus<br>Anthracnose<br>Halo blight | Parsnips | Canker |
| Blackcurrants | Mildew | Peas | Powdery mildew<br>Common wilt<br>Downy mildew<br>Enation virus<br>*Fusarium* wilt |
| Broccoli raab | Black rot<br>Downy mildew<br>Clubroot | | |
| Brussels sprouts | Leaf spot<br>Powdery mildew | Peppers | Tobacco mosaic virus |
| Carrots | Rust flies | Potatoes | Blight<br>Golden nematodes<br>Scab<br>Blackleg<br>Gangrene<br>White nematodes<br>Leaf roll |
| Corn | Rust | | |
| Cucumbers | Cucumber mosaic virus<br>Powdery mildew<br>Scab<br>Leaf spot<br>*Cladosporium* leaf mold | | |
| | | Raspberries | Aphids |
| Gooseberries | Mildew | Rutabagas | Clubroot<br>Mildew |
| Grapes | Downy mildew<br>Powdery mildew | Spinach | Mildew |
| Leeks | Rust | Tomatoes | Tobacco mosaic virus<br>*Fusarium* wilt<br>*Cladosporium* leaf mold<br>*Verticillium* wilt<br>Mildew |
| Lettuces | Root aphids<br>Mosaic virus<br>Mildew<br>Aphids | | |
| Melons | Powdery mildew<br>*Fusarium* wilt | Zucchini and summer squash | Cucumber mosaic virus<br>Powdery mildew |

# Companion planting

Companion planting is usually associated with vegetable growing, and it refers to the crops that can be combined successfully and give added benefits over simple intercropping.

Care must be taken not to crowd plants, but as long as sufficient air, light, nutrients, and water are available some combinations of crops do particularly well together. For example, instead of three areas growing, respectively, peas, potatoes, and corn, I find that growing all three crops in the three areas gives a higher total yield. On each area I grow peas in a narrow row down the center and flank the row on either side with alternate corn and potato plants. The peas provide shelter for the other young shoots, the potatoes keep the soil covered and moist, which the corn and peas enjoy, and none shades out the others.

> Combining and mixing crops significantly reduces damage from pests and diseases

In addition, combining and mixing crops significantly reduces the damage from pests and diseases. For example, I have found that beet grown between rutabagas and parsnips do not get attacked by the birds.

## Helpful herbs

• Many annual herbs are beneficial when they are grown with crops, especially as their strong scents help to hide the food plants from their pests.
• Perennial herbs, such as rosemary, thyme, sage, chives, southernwood, hyssop, and lavender, are beneficial around the edges of the vegetable garden, where their scents are effective pest-deterrents and their flowers bring in predators for the pests and pollinators for the crops.
• Most useful of all are French marigolds, which should be planted in every area and by pathways and gates so you brush against them, releasing their pungent smell.
• In the fruit garden, companion plants will compete initially but later can be of immense benefit in attracting and maintaining predators and pollinators. *Limnanthes douglasii* (poached-egg plant), *Convolvulus tricolor*, chives, nasturtiums, rosemary, thyme, and sage will all be of benefit, and clovers and alfalfa can be added to the grass-seed mixture when grassing down trees.

## Sacrificial crops

Some plants are grown to attract pests away from the main planting. They may be the same plant grown around the edge of the garden or a more attractive lure. For example, redcurrants will keep birds off the blackcurrants. In the same way, if you shred surplus leaves or seedlings when transplanting and spread the mixture around the transplants, it will fob off slugs.

Trap plants are similar to sacrificials. For example, flowering tobaccos, especially *Nicotiana sylvestris*, have sticky stems and leaves and are attractive to whiteflies and thrips. Growing these among other plants draws pests, which can then be further "stuck on" with a sugar solution spray and removed with the plant.

# Companion planting: vegetables

| Vegetable | Does well with | Does badly with |
|---|---|---|
| Beans, bush | Celery, cucurbits, potatoes, strawberries, and corn | Garlic and onions |
| Beans, fava | Brassicas, carrots, celery, cucurbits, potatoes, summer savory, and most herbs | Garlic and onions |
| Beans, pole | Corn and summer savory | Beet and chards |
| Beet and chards | Beans (most), brassicas, garlic, kohlrabi, onions, parsnips, and swedes | Pole beans |
| Brassicas and cabbage family | Beet, celery, chards, dill, garlic, nasturtiums, onions, peas, and tomatoes | Pole beans and strawberries |
| Carrots | Chives, garlic, leeks, lettuces, onions, peas, and tomatoes | |
| Celery and celeriac | Brassicas, beans, leeks, and tomatoes | |
| Corn | Beans, curcurbits, peas, and potatoes | |
| Cucurbits (cucumber, zucchini, summer and winter squashes, melon) | Beans, nasturtiums, peas, and corn | Potatoes |
| Garlic and onions | Beet, chards, lettuces, strawberries, summer savory, and tomatoes | Beans and peas |
| Leeks | Carrots, celery, and onions | |
| Lettuces | Carrots, chervil, cucurbits, radishes, and strawberries | |
| Peas | Beans, carrots, curcurbits, corn, and turnips | Garlic and onions |
| Potatoes | Beans, brassicas, peas, and corn | Cucurbits and tomatoes |
| Rutabagas and turnips | Peas | |
| Tomatoes | Asparagus, basil, carrots, garlic, onions, and parsley | Kohlrabi and potatoes |

# "Beneficial" and companion plants

Mixtures of plants are less bothered by pests than monocultures, but we can also use companions, such as aromatic herbs, deliberately to camouflage or disguise the scent of the crop. French marigolds are particularly effective; they not only hide other plants but also actually discourage and poison pests. They discourage whiteflies from coming into the greenhouse and kill nematodes in the soil. Some American gardeners grow old-fashioned varieties, as modern French marigolds have been bred to have less smell! I use golden feverfew for its strong scent and cheerful appearance. Most of the daisy family, Compositae, seem helpful in this way as well as being pretty, and they are almost all attractive to beneficial insects. The edible chrysanthemum 'Shungi-ku' is also a pungent and effective companion, keeping many pests off brassicas and related ornamentals. Almost as useful as the French marigolds are the African and Mexican forms, though these grow much bigger.

Chives and garlic are renowned as good companions for most plants. *Limnanthes douglasii*, *Phacelia tanacetifolia*, pot marigold, *Convolvolus tricolor*, and alpine strawberries are all excellent companions for bringing in beneficial

*Above: Nasturtiums are cheerful, attractive, and edible plants with beneficial effects.*

insects and some should be grown in every area. Nasturtiums are always reckoned to drive woolly aphids off apple trees and this applies to all the ornamental forms as well. Lavender under roses is a traditional companion to keep their pests away. I also find catnip works well and dies down in winter allowing the addition of thicker mulches.

## Companion plants and disease prevention

Many gardeners believe that some companion plants, such as nettles and alliums, actually help prevent fungal and bacterial attacks on other plants. Although not many of us want stinging nettles all over the garden they can be allowed in moderation in wild gardens, and they are quite good to eat when young. However, there are many

> Nasturtiums are always reckoned to drive woolly aphids off apple trees

prettier deadnettle relatives that are also good companions, flowering over a long period and much more suited to ornamental areas.

Chives and garlic are traditionally grown under roses, fruit, and ornamentals to discourage fungal and bacterial diseases, and as they are strong accumulators of sulfur there may be reason. There are many ornamental alliums that probably have similar properties and would look better—though there is little to match the flowering heads of leeks! Chamomile is said to be the plant physician and aids other plants growing nearby—anyway it smells good and makes a calming tea.

*Below: An underplanting of* Limnanthes douglasii *maintains a healthy supply of predators and pollinators in the fruit cage.*

# Companion planting in ornamental areas

Most of the good companions, such as French marigolds and aromatic herbs, that benefit fruit and vegetables also suit ornamentals. So, when planning ornamental areas of shrubs and trees, include some of those along with some evergreen shrubs and dense groundcover to give shelter and nest sites year-round. Plant deep- and shallow-rooters and include several leguminous species such as *Acacia, Cercis, Genista, Gleditsia, Spartium,* and *Cytisus.*

Likewise among herbaceous plants include a few dense evergreen clumps and mix in leguminous plants such as lupins, *Galega, Baptisia, Hedysarum,* and sweet peas.

# Basic plant care

Good methods and conditions set plants off with a flying start and keep them growing without check or hindrance. Plants that are once checked or slowed down in their growth never do as well as those that grow consistently: their tissues harden and further growth is restrained.

In many ways growing plants is a bit like looking after babies. It is critical to get them through the earliest stages, but later on they are tough enough to endure less careful treatment with little risk of permanent damage. So organic gardeners ensure freedom from early stress, and keep down the competition from weeds and other plants. This treatment produces healthy, robust plants which grow well in spite of attacks from pests and diseases, in much the same way as humans shrug off colds and scratches.

## Rotation

In the vegetable garden rotation is the most important technique (see page 82). Move the plant each year, and pests and diseases overwintering in the soil emerge to find their target has gone. The same applies to replanting and disease: never replace a dead shrubby plant with another of the same. Rotation also changes and modifies the conditions in the soil, ensuring that fewer pests or disease spores survive until the crop returns.

> In many ways growing plants is a bit like looking after babies

## Timing

Plants that are grown in season are the healthiest and survive most diseases, but there can be an advantage in early or late sowing if the crop thereby misses the worst attacks of a pest or disease. In most years, for example, early potatoes are out of the ground before blight becomes a problem. Overwintered fava beans are usually too tough early in the season for black aphids to bother them. Likewise, early-sown carrots miss rust flies, especially if they are harvested early, and late-sown ones may also avoid the pest at the end of the season.

## Pests and diseases

Indoor or undercover propagation not only helps to give plants a better early or late start and so help them to escape attacks, but can also prevent these entirely by isolating the crop during its most vulnerable stage. Beet sown in the open can be razed to the ground by birds but may survive if planted out when they are bigger.

Accurate sowing and indoor propagation also overcome the need for thinning, which can attract pests by spreading the plants' scent, as happens with carrot rust flies or onion flies.

Pruning shrubby plants in the summer is beneficial because it controls growth and so encourages flowering and fruiting. It can simultaneously remove a developing pest population, especially aphids, as these cluster on tips. During the winter months rake aside heavy mulches put down in fall. This will disturb many pests, which may be hibernating, and they will be either killed directly or through exposure to birds. This is especially useful against raspberry beetles. A heavy mulch applied before regrowth in spring seals spores and infective material beneath it. This is recommended for most plants, and is particularly effective against an attack of black spot on roses.

## Seaweed sprays

These are applied to boost growth and are also good for reducing pest and disease problems. They do not act directly as pesticides but aid the plants to make resilient, vigorous growth that throws off attacks. The smell of seaweed may also help by confusing pests.

*Above: The rose 'Zéphirine Drouhin' climbs up to meet the trailing vine, creating a shady area.*

*Below: This grass path works well with the dense leylandii hedge and acid-green feverfew border to create an enticing alleyway.*

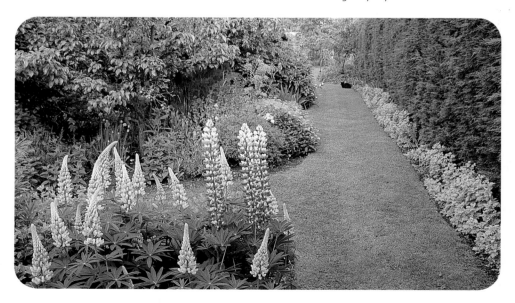

# Watering

More plants do badly through over- or underwatering than from almost all other causes together. In times of strong growth it is almost impossible to overwater plants in the open ground. Plants growing in pots in winter can be difficult to underwater. It is between these two extremes that the difficulty lies.

In the open ground try to conserve winter rains with mulches and except during droughts restrict watering to: before sowing; newly emergent seedlings; new transplants; and crops at a critical stage (usually when their flowers are setting). In times of drought, water the most valued plants with one long soak rather than everything little and often, as much of this will just evaporate. Above all, keep down weed competition and mulch well.

Do not try to wet large areas of soil around each plant as this mostly evaporates. Instead, try to soak water down to the roots. A whole, half-

> In times of drought, water the most valued plants with one long soak

*Below: Thyme enjoys a position that provides warmth at ground level combined with a cool root run.*

## Drought-resistant plants

As the climate dries and we economize on water, we need to grow fewer water-demanding plants. Rather than planting out displays of bedding plants, permanent evergreen groundcover makes more sense and the days of the lawn seem numbered. Obviously plants adapted to a Mediterranean or desert climate are mostly well suited to a no- or low-watering regime, but you could also consider those native to dry sandy soils such as the heaths and coastal plants. Herbs, especially those with silvery or gray aromatic foliage, thrive in dry, sunny conditions. Among crop plants there are few that do really well on dry soil, but perennial and deep-rooted crops, such as some fruit trees, do better than vegetables, especially figs and grapes if they are well established initially.

buried pot, or a trench beside plants that need copious watering, speeds up the task. A neat idea is to take a clear soda bottle with the bottom cut off (this can be used as a mini-cloche elsewhere). Invert the top and push it in beside a plant; a litre or two can then be poured rapidly into the funnel to trickle in slowly. A pair of watering cans with sawn-off spouts are easily carried and pour faster than those with water breakers or long narrow spouts (but always use a water breaker when watering directly onto the soil surface).

Rainwater is usually preferable to municipal water, because it is warmer coming from a rain barrel than up out of the water line, and it has fewer minerals, with no chlorine or fluoride added. However, rainwater is not sterile and it can cause damping off of young seedlings.

## Automatic watering systems

These can be as simple as a slowly filling, self-emptying cistern, a constant drip from a network of pipes, underground porous pipes, or direct feeds, or as complicated as a misting or spraying system all controlled by a timer, electrically or even by computerized remote sensors. They are quite expensive to set up and difficult to get right initially but then save a lot of time, and are of most use where the same things are being grown all the time. A simple trick for the odd plant is to stand a big container of water higher than the pot and lead a wick of a wetted, rolled-up piece of cloth from the reservoir down to the soil.

*Right: This rain barrel is made from a recycled deep freeze, which has been painted matt black.*

## Maximize your use of rainwater

You can increase your water-holding capacity by linking several barrels with siphons. One barrel on the patio by a downpipe can fill up half-a-dozen behind the shed and one in the greenhouse, and another in the vegetable garden. The barrels need to be adjusted to the same level, so that when you take water out of any one all the others fill it up again. This means that you do not need to carry water around the garden as much: it is waiting for you.

# Step 5 Encourage wildlife

Organic gardeners want as many types of wildlife as possible. The more forms of life, the more they control each other and the more fertilizer rains down on our crops. Not only that but they are interesting and beautiful to observe, too. Moreover if we encourage small things then bigger ones survive. I'm sorry for the bird taken by the hawk but it was fantastic to see—and only the summer before I saw a bird eat a newt!

## How to attract wildlife

It is easy to provide wildlife with a wide variety of food—it is called a garden; but our overtidiness in the garden has eliminated too many of the nooks and crannies where wildlife lives and, as with birds' nests, we need artificial alternatives. Obviously a dovecote needs to be decorative as well as functional, but on the smaller scale our provision for birds can be very humble and of recycled materials as the nests are so small and easily hidden.

The smallest creatures hibernate inside dry bundles of sticks and under piles of stones. Water and damp places are essential for others; a pile of rotting logs beside a pool, for example, will attract beetles to lay their eggs.

*Above: Foxgloves and an old rotting log provide shelter for wildlife and an attractive wild corner.*

# Water in the garden

Water in any form will give a lot of pleasure and is almost essential in an organic garden: even a tiny pond adds to the atmosphere and is also wonderfully attractive to wildlife. Birds, insects, and animals all need water and will come to your garden if you supply it; once there, they help with pest control. Also, if water is more accessible, birds eat less fruit. A bird bath can be fitted into every garden—ideally where it can be seen from a window and is safe from cats. A fountain or cascade, however humble, is a delight and can be combined with a pond (though waterlilies like still water). Ponds do not have to be large to attract wildlife, provided they never dry up. Even an old bath set in the ground will do well. All water

*Above: The honey-scented* Buddleja globosa *is good for attracting insects.*

needs a sloping edge to let creatures in and out, and secure fencing if young children are around.

In a large garden you could have ponds in different areas to make different ecosystems. Large ponds create microclimates that can shelter tender plants nearby, and they reflect sunlight onto surrounding plants as well as providing an emergency source of water.

When making a pond, line it with newspaper and old carpet first to prevent the liner being punctured on stones. Similarly lay old carpet upside down over the edges to protect the liner from light and wear, so that it lasts longer. E.P.D.M. is the best-value synthetic rubber liner as it lasts longer, but the cheaper alternatives are just as good if well protected. Fill the pond and let it stand for a week to warm up and lose chlorine before stocking it. Take a bucket to a "natural" pond and scoop up some mud and water for an instant ecosystem.

> Ponds do not have to be large to attract wildlife

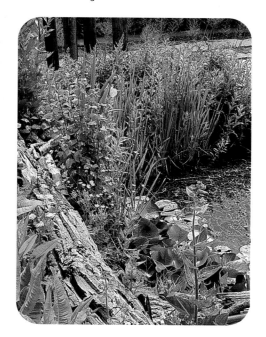

*Above: A pond is important in an organic garden because it provides a habitat for lots of wildlife.*

# Nooks, crannies, nests, and hedges

As well as providing food, it is well worth adding places for beneficial wild animals to rest, hibernate, or lay eggs. If you think about the natural sites they prefer, it will give you ideas about what to add.

## Hidey-holes

Frogs, newts, and toads are encouraged primarily by a pool or pond but they also spend much of their lives on land. In the winter they prefer damp, frost-free places, ideally damp burrows beside a pond that are well insulated from above and just above the highest floodline! These burrows can easily be created with old drainage pipes, bricks, and stones and covered with a layer of soil and sod.

Piles of decaying logs and bark provide a multitude of resources and are especially useful as low walls around ponds where they also prevent children and herons from gaining easy access. Such piles may be accused of harboring pests and diseases such as honey fungus. However, I have never seen evidence of a pile initiating such an attack, while freshly killed tree stumps have often.

## Nests and hibernation sites

Piles of stones, bricks, tiles, and even bottles are also useful to many small creatures for nest and hibernation sites and these can be hidden under hedges and large shrubs. (Bottles must be positioned neck down or filled with sticks or they are deadfall traps.) Even piles of sand left undisturbed soon get colonized by many interesting insects, and creating a sandy bank will bring in some rarities.

Hedges, especially dense and evergreen ones, provide lots of niches for creatures to live in. Mixed informal hedges provide variety but a neat formal hedge has a dry internal space that can be filled with nest and hibernation sites. The ground underneath can be thickly mulched with the hedge's own prunings, in most cases with little risk of disease, and this will attract many creatures.

## Lacewing hotels and ladybeetle refuges

Lacewings and ladybeetles are some of the garden's most important pollinators and predators. You can help these beneficial insects by providing them with winter quarters. You can make your own out of bundles of hollow stems. These can be simply tied, or made more weatherproof by inserting them in a tube cut from a plastic soda bottle, then hidden out of sight inside dense and evergreen shrubs, trees, and hedges. Even bundles of thorny prunings can be utilized this way to make snug refuges for these insects.

# Attracting beneficial insects

Building up self-regulating ecosystems means making good provision for predators—incorporating plants to provide nectar, fruits, and pollen; shelter on the large and small scale; sites for nests and hibernation quarters; an accessible and reliable water supply; and sacrificial plants to breed up pests on which the predators and parasites can be maintained.

Companion plants that encourage predators should ideally keep flowering throughout the whole season and particularly early on in the year. Not all flowers are equally useful though: deep-throated flowers intended for moths and butterflies, and double flowers which have been specially bred for their beauty at the cost of nectar, are less effective.

Of all beneficial insects, flower flies are probably the most important, and they are attracted to *Limnanthes douglasii* (poached-egg plant) in particular. This can be grown as a self-seeding annual under roses, shrubs, and fruit. Ladybeetles, lacewings, and predatory wasps are attracted to the same flowers as flower flies but also like alliums, anthemis, fennel, and yarrow. Aphids will seek out patches of nettles, honeysuckles, sweet cherries, and lupines, which then maintain a background level of predators and parasites.

> Double flowers specially bred for their beauty at the cost of nectar are less effective

*Above: Buddleja is worth growing for the beautiful Peacock butterflies it attracts.*

*Below: The aphids on this foxglove appear to be doing no harm and are distracted from plants that they might really damage.*

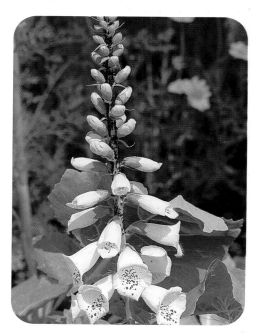

# Attracting beneficial insects

## Plants for insects and wildlife

| Plant | Animals attracted | | | | | |
|---|---|---|---|---|---|---|
| | Flower flies | Bees | Lady-beetles | Lace-wings | Butter-flies | Birds |
| *Achillea millefolium* (common yarrow) | ✓ | ✓ | ✓ | ✓ | | |
| *Ajuga reptans* (common bugle) | | ✓ | | | | |
| *Allium schoenoprasum* (chives) | | ✓ | | | | |
| *Anchusa azurea* (Italian bugloss) | | ✓ | | | | |
| *Anethum graveolens* (dill) | ✓ | | | | | |
| *Angelica archangelica* (Norwegian angelica) | ✓ | | | | | |
| *Anthemis* | | | | ✓ | | |
| *Arabis caucasica* (alpine rockcress) | | ✓ | | | | |
| *Bergenia* | ✓ | | | | | |
| *Borago officinalis* (common borage) | | ✓ | | | | |
| *Buddleja davidii* | | | | ✓ | ✓ | |
| *Calendula* (marigold) | ✓ | | ✓ | | | |
| *Campanula* | | ✓ | | | | |
| *Centaurea* | ✓ | | | | | |
| *Centranthus ruber* (red valerian) | | ✓ | | | ✓ | |
| *Convolvulus tricolor* | ✓ | | | ✓ | | |
| *Coreopsis grandiflora* (large flower tickseed) | | ✓ | | | | |
| *Cosmos* | ✓ | ✓ | | ✓ | | |
| *Delphinium* | | ✓ | | | | |
| *Digitalis* (foxglove) | | ✓ | | | | |
| *Dipsacus fullonum* (Fuller's teasel) | | ✓ | | | ✓ | ✓ |
| *Echinops ritro* | | ✓ | | | | |
| *Eryngium* (eryngo) | | ✓ | | | | |
| *Erysimum* (wallflower) | | ✓ | | | | |
| *Eschscholzia californica* | | ✓ | | | | |
| *Filipendula ulmaria* (queen of the meadow) | | | | | | ✓ |
| *Foeniculum vulgare* (fennel) | ✓ | ✓ | ✓ | | | |
| *Geranium* (cranesbill) | | | | | | ✓ |
| *Gypsophila* (baby's breath) | | ✓ | | | ✓ | |
| *Helianthus* (sunflower) | | ✓ | | | ✓ | ✓ |
| *Heliotropium arborescens* (garden heliotrope) | | | | | ✓ | |
| *Hyssopus officinalis* (hyssop) | | ✓ | | | | |
| *Iberis* (candytuft) | | | | | ✓ | |

# Plants for insects and wildlife

| Plant | Animals attracted | | | | | |
|---|---|---|---|---|---|---|
| | Flower flies | Bees | Lady-beetles | Lace-wings | Butter-flies | Birds |
| *Lamium album* (white deadnettle) | | ✓ | | | | |
| *Lavandula* (lavender) | | ✓ | | | | |
| *Lavatera* (tree mallow) | | ✓ | | | | |
| *Leucanthemum x superbum* (shasta daisy) | ✓ | | | | | |
| *Levisticum officinale* (garden lovage) | ✓ | | | | | |
| *Limnanthes douglasii* (poached-egg plant) | ✓ | ✓ | | | | |
| *Lobularia maritima* (sweet alyssum) | | ✓ | | | ✓ | |
| *Lonicera* (honeysuckle) | | ✓ | | | ✓ | |
| *Lunaria annua* (honesty) | | | | | ✓ | ✓ |
| *Lysimachia punctata* (yellow loosestrife) | | ✓ | | | | |
| *Melissa officinalis* (common balm) | | | | | | |
| *Mentha* (mint) | | ✓ | | | ✓ | |
| *Monarda didyma* | | ✓ | | | ✓ | |
| *Muscari* (grape hyacinth) | | ✓ | | | | |
| *Myosotis* (forget-me-not) | | ✓ | | | | |
| *Myrrhis odorata* | ✓ | | | | | |
| *Nepeta* (catnip) | | ✓ | | | ✓ | |
| *Origanum vulgare* (marjoram) | | ✓ | | | ✓ | |
| *Papaver* (poppy) | | ✓ | | | | |
| *Phacelia tanacetifolia* | ✓ | ✓ | | | | |
| *Pyracantha* (firethorn) | | | | | | ✓ |
| *Reseda odorata* (garden mignonette) | | ✓ | | | ✓ | |
| *Ribes* (flowering currant) | | ✓ | | | | |
| *Rosmarinus officinalis* (rosemary) | | ✓ | | | | |
| *Rudbeckia* | ✓ | | | | | |
| *Saponaria officinalis* (bouncing bet) | | | | | ✓ | |
| *Sedum spectabile* (showy stonecrop) | | ✓ | | | ✓ | |
| *Solidago* (goldenrod) | ✓ | ✓ | | ✓ | | |
| *Symphytum officinale* (common comfrey) | | ✓ | | | | |
| *Tagetes* (marigold) | ✓ | | | | | |
| *Thymus* (thyme) | | ✓ | | | | |
| *Trifolium* (clover) | | ✓ | | | | |

# Encouraging beneficial birds

Birds are most easily increased by the provision of bird houses as suitable sites are now rare. It is important to encourage the most useful birds: blue tits, great tits, tree sparrows, and other small insectivorous birds need little wooden boxes about 5–6in. (13–15cm) all round with a hole at the front of 1¾in. (4cm). Robins, wagtails, and flycatchers prefer the box to have a bigger opening, of 2 x 3in. (5 x 7.5cm). These resemble natural nesting holes and should be fixed to trees where cats and other predators cannot get at them. Put them where you can watch from a window, except those for robins, which like boxes to be well hidden away in shrubs or hedges. Many other birds, such as blackbirds and thrushes, find ample nest sites in dense evergreens or thick hedges. You can also encourage birds by providing a supply of water, feeding them kitchen scraps, or wild bird seed on a platform bird feeder, and fitting berry-carrying shrubs into the garden.

## Food for birds

The simplest way to provide food for birds is, of course, to put out peanuts (make sure they are aflatoxin free) and wild bird seed. When you are designing your garden, it is worth thinking about where such items as platform bird feeders and birdbaths will be positioned. This is not a problem with free-standing ones, but if you want a suspended bird feeder you will have to give the siting more thought. From the birds' point of view, it does not much matter where the feeding station is, as long as it is safe from surprise attacks from cats or dogs. If you want to enjoy watching birds as they feed, consider placing the bird feeder where it can be seen easily from a window.

Berries and seeds represent the major part of many birds' diets, and these can be provided by including shrubs and other plants that bear berries in the garden. Small trees, including *Sorbus* (rowan) and *Ilex aquifolium* (holly), bear berries that are greatly enjoyed by birds in winter. Perennial plants are also a useful source of seeds. Many birds, notably goldfinches, will visit gardens in large numbers to feed on seedheads that have been left. Leaving old vegetation standing throughout winter can make a garden look rather unkempt and untidy, but it is worth leaving at least some through the cold months. The old vegetation is a hiding place for many insects, and insectivorous birds will come seeking food.

*Below: The handsome red berries of* Berberis thunbergii *will attract birds to your garden.*

# Trees and shrubs for berries

| Plant | Features |
|---|---|
| *Berberis thunbergii* (Japanese barberry) | A deciduous shrub with bright red berries in winter |
| *Cotoneaster horizontalis* | Red winter berries attract all kinds of birds |
| *Crataegus monogyna* (oneseed hawthorn) | Glossy, dark red berries provide food for many species in winter |
| *Hedera helix* (English ivy) | Fall and winter berries are an important food for lots of birds |
| *Ilex aquifolium* (English holly) | The red fall and winter berries are especially appreciated by birds |
| *Leycesteria formosa* (Himalayan honeysuckle) | In fall red-purple berries attract birds to your garden |
| *Lonicera periclymenum* (European honeysuckle) | Glossy red fall berries are enjoyed by lots of birds |
| *Pyracantha* 'Orange Glow' | Vivid orange fruits in fall to winter are appreciated by garden birds |
| *Sambucus racemosa* (red elderberry) | Many species will eat the fall fruits |
| *Sorbus aria* (chess-apple) | The colorful berries are a valuable food for birds in the fall |

# Grow organic

Vegetables and fruit need the best possible conditions, which means growing them in a deep, rich soil that has been well fed with organic material. If the soil is poor, you will have to do a great deal of work before it is worthwhile even trying to grow food crops.

## The vegetable garden

Ideally, the area should be in full sun, with no overhanging trees. Wet, boggy sites and low ground should be avoided, as they will result in winter losses and frost damage in spring. The vegetable garden should not be too far from the kitchen, a water source, and the garden shed, or much time will be wasted going to and fro.

### Crop rotation

It is critical is that you do not grow the same crop, or a near relation, on the same piece of ground year after year. Move the crop around or leave it out entirely for a year or two. What follows what is not that important, although some combinations can be less satisfactory—potatoes do not happily follow brassicas or legumes if the soil was limed for them, for example—but it is important to make sure that you do not replant potatoes, tomatoes, and brassicas in the same spot for as many years as possible, and that other vegetables are not grown on the same site as the year before.

Of course, the more elaborate your rotation and the longer the gaps, the better the results, and this is easier if you grow a wider variety of crops in smaller amounts, and if you introduce "break crops," such as flowers, strawberries or artichokes, to the plot for a few years.

### Row or block planting

Block and row planting are alternative ways of laying out crops. Those that need support, such as peas, are better in rows that run north–south, so that the ground between is not shaded. Rows are not essential, however: you can even grow beans and peas in a circle by attaching a wheel to the top of a pole and running strings down from it. Rows waste a lot of space and the paths between them get compacted and need digging. For most crops, especially those that are close planted, such as carrots, block planting is better. Apart from saving space and reducing digging, it helps with weed control, because once the plants are half-grown their foliage meets, excluding light from the soil and choking out weed seedlings. This also forms a favorable microclimate and prevents moisture loss. If netting or floating row cover is used to prevent pests reaching the plants, block planting is again more practical. For successful block planting you need loose, deep soil to enable the roots to go deeper in search of nutrients.

## Raised beds

Many of the advantages of raised beds come from their being fixed. They are simply permanent sub-plots surrounded by narrow paths. The beds are not walked on, so need digging only every seven or eight years, and they make block planting easy, although rows can still be run down the middle if the beds run north–south. The ideal width is about 4ft. (1.2m), which is comfortable to reach from either side, and they should be no longer than about 16ft. (5m), or you will be tempted to walk over rather than around them. Having permanently fixed beds makes record-keeping and thus crop rotation a simple process.

Fixed beds slowly become raised beds naturally as mulches, compost, and root residues build up.

As well as making them less back-breaking to work, raising the soil level has several advantages. As the bed builds up, the surface area increases, not only giving some extra planting space but also increasing aeration and evaporation. They give an earlier start in spring because the soil warms up sooner; and in winter the crops on top are in slightly warmer conditions as cold air runs off to lower levels. However, raised beds also dry out more quickly in summer, and mulches tend to slide off or be pulled off by birds.

> The vegetable garden should not be too far from the kitchen

On the whole, the advantages outweigh the problems, especially if their shape is kept to the natural curve formed by the soil. This provides several useful microclimates. In a bed running north–south, the sunny end is a hot slope, suitable for early cropping and tender herbs, while the shaded end suits salad and leafy greens. The sides are protected from the wind and thus stay moist, suiting leeks, roots, and salad greens. The top is open ground, but especially well suited to onions, shallots, brassicas, and legumes grown in rows and for overwintering vegetables.

Paths of compacted soil are sufficient but get muddy in the wet. Builder's sand or crushed gravel is more suitable and it doesn't matter if some gets mixed into the soil.

Raising beds artificially with boards, bricks, or a similar material around the sides reduces the area available for planting, removes many of the useful microclimates, adds to costs, and provides hiding places for pests.

# Growing in a greenhouse

A greenhouse is a great boon for raising plants and extending the growing season. Greenhouses come in sizes to suit most budgets and gardens, and are worthwhile as an aid to gardening, but they can take up a lot of time and money if you fill them with tender plants in pots. The smaller the garden, the more valuable greenhouse space will be, as it enables you to start off plants for later planting as beds become vacant.

A greenhouse needs to be near the house for access and services but is also difficult to site attractively because screening may rob it of light. In many ways a sunroom may be a more practical solution and saves siting a greenhouse within view of the house. Water nearby is essential, and electric light and power will allow evening work and the use of thermostatic propagation, further increasing the value of the greenhouse. Wooden greenhouses are slightly easier on the eye than metal-framed ones and tend to be warmer. Extra plastic insulation is a mixed blessing, because although it keeps greenhouses warmer it reduces the light. Ventilation must be adequate and automatic, unless you are at home all day.

## Organic management under cover

Growing under walk-in cover, whether in the form of a greenhouse or hoop house, is an artificial method of gardening, and it requires more intervention because the natural systems cannot control pests and diseases, the temperature may rise too far, and rain does not fall.

There are two main approaches:

1. A "sterile environment" approach involves cleaning the greenhouse thoroughly, using a high-pressure water or steam jet, and treating the plants only if they are subject to any attack using some of the methods described on pages 31 and 33. This method resembles the conventional approach to gardening.

## Hoop houses

Hoop houses are less visually appealing than greenhouses, but they are ideal for a large garden because they give a lot of space for the money and are easy to move. They need to be well ventilated, as they are prone to high humidity which can promote fungal diseases. The cover will need replacing every four years or so, when the house can be moved to a different piece of ground—the vegetable bed is convenient because it can then be incorporated into the crop rotation.

2. The alternative is to try to build up semi-natural systems, concentrating more on using predators for pest control.
• Water in saucers, nests of straw-filled pots, and groundcover plants can be included under benches and in shady corners for beetles, frogs, and toads.
• Ladybeetles, spiders, and bought-in predators, such as those outlined on page 33, can be

*Above: The external appearance of the hoop house is much improved by growing vines and lush herbs immediately outside.*

*Below:* Nicotiana sylvestris *has sticky leaves which trap any whiteflies and thrips that the marigolds at the entrance fail to discourage.*

introduced and encouraged with rolled-up cardboard nests tied in dry nooks and crannies. With this approach, even organic pesticides cannot be used, because the natural predators will suffer, but companion plants can be used. It is beneficial to grow French marigolds in the greenhouse or hoop house, especially by the door where you brush against them and release their scent, because they keep out whiteflies but attract bees and flower flies. *Nicotiana* especially *N. sylvestris* (South American tobacco) is also beneficial because their sticky stems trap many little insects, such as thrips.

It is preferable to grow plants to fruition directly in the soil rather than in containers, because it saves on watering and compost. Even with rotation, moving the plants around each year and adding copious amounts of garden compost, however, yields start to drop after five years or so. The answer is simply to dig out the topsoil and replace it with compost and fresh soil dug from a clean part of the garden. This is hard work but does not need doing often and is less work than filling up and watering loads of containers every year.

> Remember that fruit grown under cover will need pollinating by hand

Old carpet and cardboard can be used to cover bare soil in greenhouses and hoop houses and makes rather effective paths. This prevents weeds germinating and minimizes moisture loss, stops splashing of soil onto crops, is more pleasant to work on, and when the strips are rolled back makes it easy to pick off slugs and other pests hiding there.

# Vegetables

A greenhouse is not needed for starting off hardy vegetables in cells or pots as they will be more than happy in a cold frame or sheltered spot until they are ready to go out. However, a greenhouse does make it easier to provide better conditions earlier, especially enough light and warmth, and this can then be used later for growing tender crops to fruition. Cloches are nearly as good but do not have as much space and are difficult to use, and while hoop houses give the best value for money they are not nice to look at. Whatever you choose, be careful to keep the glass or plastic clean, as light is more important than heat for most plants, especially hardy vegetables. Ventilation is also important as it is easy to cook small seedlings if the full sun comes out on them while they are tightly sealed up—either be vigilant or invest in an automatic vent opener.

Once hardy vegetables have started growing well in pots, then they can be planted out, but they must be hardened off first. This simply means getting them used to tougher conditions by

## Greenhouse hygiene

Common greenhouse diseases are mildew, blight, botrytis, and leaf spot (see pages 44–9). In general, they can be controlled by maintaining strict hygiene in the greenhouse, and any diseased or damaged plants should be removed immediately. Good ventilation is essential to prevent plants suffering from moisture or heat stress.

standing them outside each day, but putting them back under cover at night for three or four days. Do not skimp on this important exercise unless cloches or clear plastic soda bottles are used to protect plants when they are first put outside, in which case they can be planted out with a little less initial hardening off.

# Fruit

In colder regions tender crops, including tropical fruit, can be grown in the greenhouse. This gives excellent bird and frost protection and earlier crops, but on the down side tends to cause more pest and disease problems. There is no background ecology of predators and parasites, and diseases tend to spread more easily in the close, often humid conditions inside.

To combat pests try companion planting of flowers, such as *Tagetes* (French marigolds), which attract aphid predators. Alternatively, spray with soft soap or use biological pest control of whiteflies and red spider mites by introducing parasites (see page 33).

*Right: The large plant in the doorway is* Nicandra physalodes *(apple of Peru) which discourages whiteflies from attacking valuable food crops.*

Fruits can be grown either in border soil or in containers in a greenhouse. The advantage of using containers in the greenhouse is that this restricts growth more easily than pruning. It also enables plants to be stood outside for the summer months, but they will then require even more careful watering. Container growing in a greenhouse is most suitable for grapes, peaches, and citrus fruits. Remember that fruit grown under cover will need pollinating by hand.

# Growing in containers

One advantage of containers is that you are free to choose a potting soil to suit the plants you wish to grow. Ordinary soil is too poor for most plants confined in a pot and a strong soil-based mix should be used. Peat-based potting mixes (see pages 12–13) are really too light for containers and the best substitute is a soil-based one (except for acidic-lovers). This can be mixed with other ingredients such as leafmold and rotted sods for really large containers but do not economize when filling small pots; plants need good stuff if they are to do well. I use sifted garden compost for potting most subjects and always for the bigger and tougher plants.

Do not mulch plants in pots as it stops the soil breathing, though a thin layer of builder's sand or gravel suppresses weeds and reduces splashing. Plants in containers need careful feeding with well-diluted liquid fertilizers, and perennials also need topdressing and repotting every year or so. Be diligent with regular watering otherwise they'll do badly, and conversely be careful not to let their drainage become poor and drown them.

> Do not mulch plants in pots as it stops the soil breathing

## Vegetables and herbs

It is possible to grow almost any vegetable in a suitable container but it has to be very deep for root vegetables such as maincrop carrots and parsnips, and some crops such as long-season potatoes are hardly worth the space. However, choice favorites are worth having and given enough sun, soil, and water can be grown. The smaller plants are obviously easier.

### Good choices
• Radishes, scallions, shallots, onions, garlic, lettuces, beet and bush beans are all very straightforward container subjects.
• Short, stumpy sorts of carrots are generally more successful than larger ones.
• Vines and ramblers such as gourds, cucumbers, and pole beans can be grown if they are kept well watered.
• Herbs are particularly appropriate for containers as they are mostly small and are used in small amounts yet are expensive to buy. Moreover, most can be taken indoors for the cold months and kept on a sunny windowsill.

## Fruit

In the smallest gardens it is still possible to grow fruit trees, soft fruit, and even vines, by confining them in containers. This cramps the root system, preventing them from getting too big, and tends to bring them into fruit earlier and means that much less pruning is required than for soil-grown plants. However, they are prone to dropping their fruit and even dying unless extremely good care is taken to keep them well and regularly watered—this can mean three or four times a day in summer. Similarly, attention is needed to prevent the roots freezing in winter. An advantage of container culture is that the whole pot can be taken under cover to prevent frost or bird damage or to bring on earlier growth.

Use the biggest container you can manage—trash containers can be converted with holes in the base and are much cheaper than pots. Fill with a good potting soil, use the most dwarfing rootstock, and arrange some form of automatic watering system.

### Good choices

- Sweet and sour cherries
- Peaches
- Apricots and nectarines
- Figs
- Grapes

*Right: It is possible to grow grapevines in containers, which is problem free as long as you do not neglect the watering, especially in warm weather.*

*Below: Many herbs are suitable for containers. They can be taken indoors in the winter months to prolong the harvest season.*

# Vegetables

Vegetables need the best possible conditions to give good crops: rich soil, plenty of sunlight, regular water, and unchecked growing time. Remember never to crowd plants too closely together, making them compete for nutrients, light, and water.

## Roots and tubers

### Beet

Easy to grow and highly nutritious, beet likes a deep, rich soil, so dig in well-rotted compost or manure. Sow in pots or cells under cover in early spring. Plant out or sow seeds in the open in midspring to early summer, 1in. (2.5cm) deep and 8in. (20cm) apart each way. Plants also grow well sown one seed capsule to a pot or cell and left unthinned when planting out to give little beets for pickling. Sown direct and thinned, they can be grown larger for winter storage. Avoid damaging the roots when weeding because they will bleed. Beet is trouble free, but birds eat the leaves, so protect plants with netting or black cotton.

• The yellow cultivar 'Burpee's Golden' can be recommended.

• 'Boltardy' is a round red cultivar suitable for early sowing.

• The barrel-shaped types of beet are good for slicing and storage.

• For pickling, try to find 'Crosby's Egyptian'.

### Carrots

Carrots need a light, stone-free soil to do well; lighten heavy clay soil with organic material and builder's sand. When you are digging in compost, make sure it is well rotted and friable to prevent roots from forking.

*Above: The conventional red beet on the right and the yellow 'Burpee's Golden' on the left.*

*Above: It is worth trying many different carrot varieties. This one is called 'Amsterdam Forcing'.*

Sow at three-week intervals, about 1¾in. (4cm) deep, from early spring to midsummer. Spot sowing every 6in. (15cm) is best if you want large carrots to store, but for baby carrots scatter the seed. Rake the soil then water it thoroughly; let the water drain away. Mix the seed with sand and sow this, side to side and backwards and forwards. Cover the seed with ½in. (1cm) of used sterile potting soil mixed with builder's sand. Carrots can be sown and intercropped with scallions and leeks, all sown together.

The main problem is carrot rust flies, and carrots must be grown under an old net curtain, floating row cover, or fine netting to prevent damage. Peg down the netting immediately after sowing.

There are many worthwhile cultivars.
• 'Amsterdam Forcing' is a good, quick carrot.
• 'Nantes 2' can be sown from late winter under cover right through to late summer for little ones in winter.
• 'Mokum' is a good summer carrot.
• 'Autumn King' is reliable, but a bit coarse, for winter storage.
• Roundish ones like 'Parmex' are good for shallow soils and containers.

## Jerusalem artichokes

These plants, which get to 6–8ft. (1.8–2.5m) tall, can be useful as quick, easy-to-grow windbreaks. However, they are difficult to eradicate, so are best confined to wild corners of the garden. Do not plant them where they are likely to overshadow other crops, and do not plant them unless you are sure you like them.

They will grow in poor soil, but for best results dig a trench, working in well-rotted manure or compost. Plant tubers 6in. (15cm) deep and 2ft.

(60cm) apart in each direction. Water in dry weather. Jerusalem artichokes generally seem to be immune to virtually all pests and diseases.
• Try 'Fuseau', a smooth-skinned cultivar, which is easy to prepare.

## Kohlrabi

Although rarely grown, this is easy and highly nutritious. It is rather like a turnip, and can be eaten cooked or, better, raw. It will grow in relatively poor conditions, although it prefers a rich, well-drained soil and can be transplanted from a seedbed, cells, or pots. Sow 1in. (2.5cm) deep and plant out, 10in. (25cm) apart each way, from midspring to late summer. Water well in dry weather and mulch to conserve moisture.

Kohlrabi is usually trouble free, although plants will become hard and woody if they are checked while growing. Make sure they always have sufficient water and food.
• The cultivar 'Purple Vienna' is widely available, but 'Superschmelz' is better, remaining crisp and tender while growing very large.

*Above: Kohlrabi is useful as a quick-growing, trouble-free catch crop.*

### Parsnips and turnip-rooted parsley

These roots take up the ground for a long time, and they cannot be recommended for gardens with limited space. They like well-drained soil but not one that has been recently manured. Avoid stony soil. Parsnips require spot sowing: sow three seeds 1in. (2.5cm) deep and 4in. (10cm) apart each way for small types and 10in. (25cm) apart for larger types. Sow from late winter to early spring, but not in cold, wet conditions. It is often better to wait and make a later sowing in midspring when the soil is warmer. Parsnip seed is slow to germinate and it does not keep, so use fresh each year. Thin to one seedling when they emerge and forget about them until the leaves die down, when they can be harvested.

Turnip-rooted parsley produces a parsniplike root. It tastes of parsley but is grown and used like parsnips. The leaves can be used like parsley.

Canker can be a problem with some cultivars. Avoid hoeing too close to the roots because damage to the shoulder can encourage canker. Carrot rust flies may be troublesome (see page 39). Water parsnips and turnip-rooted parsley regularly in dry weather to stop the roots from splitting.

- 'Avonresister' is good but small.
- 'Tender and True' is the best large parsnip.

### Potatoes

Although they are easy to grow, potatoes need some care to give worthwhile yields. The soil must be enriched with organic material, and they can involve a lot of work.

Because they are susceptible to diseases spread on seed potato tubers, it's best to buy new certified stock every year. However, it's possible to grow self-saved tubers for a couple of years and then to buy new stock before yields drop or after a year troubled with disease. Save only tubers from healthy, typical plants; never save from plants that yield badly or look poor; egg-sized tubers are best; green bits do not matter.

As soon as you can each year, chit the seed by laying the tubers rose-end up in a tray, keeping them in a slightly warm, well-lit place to grow short green shoots. As soon as shoots begin to grow, plant out the tubers. Early potatoes need to be 4–6in. (10–15cm) deep and 12–18in. (30–45cm) apart each way, rose-end up; mid- and long-season potatoes need the same depth but 2ft. (60cm) apart each way. To produce many small, new potatoes, leave all the shoots on; for fewer, bigger tubers remove all shoots but one. To increase yields significantly water heavily when the flowers appear and remove the poisonous seedheads that follow.

Conventionally, the seed potato is planted in a trench. I prefer to make large, saucepan-shaped holes at the required distance, using a trowel. Add comfrey leaves to the hole, followed by sifted garden compost. Plant the seed potatoes and add some grass clippings as protection against scab. Replace the soil in the hole and firm down. Once the potatoes emerge, drag soil up around each plant to molehill size. A mulch of straw, leaves, or grass clippings keeps the soil moist and protects young tubers from the sun, which would turn them green. For mid- and long-season potatoes apply a collar of newspaper under the mulch so that even if the birds scratch away the grass or straw the tubers remain out of the light.

Organic gardeners are advised to grow early potatoes. These give lower yields but crop quickly and can be harvested before potato blight can become a problem; it usually comes after midsummer during warm, wet weather. Mid-season potatoes miss most blight attacks. The more productive long-season potatoes need to grow on into early fall to give full yields. Scabby patches can be avoided by mixing grass cuttings with the soil and compost. Potatoes are also affected by wireworms, nematodes and blackleg (see pages 42–3 and 45).

There are hundreds of potatoes but only a few are widely available.
• 'Sutton's Foremost', 'Epicure', 'Sharpe's Express' and 'Pink Duke of York' are good early potatoes.
• 'Wilja' and 'Charlotte' are both good mid- and long-season potatoes.
• 'King Edward', although low-yielding, is a good long-season potato.
• 'Pink Fir Apple' is good for salads.
• 'Romano' is good for baking and chipping.

## Radishes
Sow radishes anywhere you like, a few seeds at a time, every week from spring to fall. Water in dry weather. They will tolerate most soils and are quick-growing, although they must be eaten when young and tender. Black Spanish and Japanese radishes are sown after midsummer and are more like turnips (and treated as such). Flea beetles can be a problem (see page 40).
• Try 'Cherry Belle' and 'Long White Icicle'.

## Rutabagas and turnips
Both these need a well-drained soil that is rich in humus to retain moisture. Turnips can be started in cells if they are planted out while still small, but they do best if sown direct from early spring to late summer, 1in. (2.5cm) deep and 6in. (15cm) apart each way. Keep well watered and mulch to conserve moisture. They will be tough and stringy if grown in dry conditions. Sow rutabagas in mid- to late spring, either direct or in cells, and transplant while small to 12in. (30cm) apart each way. Water well, especially in dry weather, or they will be woody. Mulch around the plants to conserve moisture.
• The best all-round turnip is 'Golden Ball', which stores reasonably well in a cool place.
• 'Snowball' is quick to grow and succulent.
• 'Acme Purple Top' and 'Marian' are recommended rutabagas.

## Salsify and black salsify
Like parsnips, these prefer deep, rich soil. Grow them like parsnips, sowing three seeds to a spot in mid- to late spring, 1in. (2.5cm) deep and 6in. (15cm) apart each way. Thin to one seedling. Weed by hand because the roots are easily damaged. Water regularly, especially in dry weather, and mulch to conserve moisture. To produce young shoots in spring, cut off the leaves in fall and hill the soil to a depth of 6in. (15cm). These should be trouble free as long as they are watered regularly.
• Try 'Mammoth' for salsify and 'Maxima' varieties for black salsify.

*Below: Turnips become tough in dry conditions, so mulch the soil to retain moisture.*

# Onion family

## Garlic and shallots

As long as you have a sunny site and have dug in plenty of well-rotted manure or compost, these are easy to grow. Both can be grown in any spare patch in the ornamental garden, where they will discourage pests and diseases in other plants.

Garlic can be planted from midfall to late winter; the earlier the better. Plant individual cloves, pointed end up, 1in. (2.5cm) deep and 6in. (15cm) apart each way. Shallots need shallow holes. Plant ½in. (1cm) deep and 9in. (23cm) apart each way from midwinter to early spring. Keep the plants weeded at all times, working by hand if necessary.

Both may be pulled out of their holes by birds or worms and will need replanting, but they are otherwise trouble free.

• The garlic 'Long Keeper' is a good variety for cooler climates.

*Above: Garlic should be harvested in the summer when the leaves begin to yellow. Loosen bulbs with a fork and leave to dry and ripen in the sun.*

## Leeks

Leeks take up little space and will do well in a rich, moist soil, although they will not do as well in hot, dry conditions. Dig in plenty of well-rotted compost or manure before planting. Sow 1in. (2.5cm) deep under cover in early spring. Plant out in late spring, 6in. (15cm) apart each way, and when transplanting use a dibble to make holes at least 6in. (15cm) deep. Insert the leek, and water in well with dilute seaweed solution. Do not fill in the holes with soil. Hoe to keep down weeds and water regularly in dry weather. Mulch to conserve moisture.

Leeks are relatively trouble free. 'Alvito' and 'Conora' are partly rust-resistant (see page 48).

• For fall leeks try 'The Lyon' or 'Argenta'.

• For winter use grow 'Musselburgh'.

• 'Alaska' will stand and grow larger until late spring; it can be grown in ornamental areas.

## Onions

Onions like a richly organic soil, so in winter be sure to dig plenty of well-rotted manure or compost into the soil. They also prefer a sunny site. Keep young onions weeded, and water regularly in dry weather.

Onion sets are easy but are more expensive than seed. However, they give good results and avoid the problems associated with seed-grown plants. Sets are planted from late winter to midspring, but the earlier the better if the ground is ready. Rake to a fine texture, then plant in shallow holes, 8in. (20cm) apart each way, and keep putting them back when the birds and worms pull them up. Sets are convenient for intercropping where space is available, especially between brassicas and in ornamental areas of the garden, where they discourage pests and diseases.

Onion seed can be sown direct, but it is better to sow under cover in mid- to late winter in pots or cells. Don't worry about getting more than one plant per cell because two or three grown together will give smaller, harder onions that keep well. Harden off for a few days in a cold frame before planting. Plant out in early to midspring, close planting at 4in. (10cm) apart each way for small, long-keeping onions and spacing to 7in. (18cm) apart each way for larger ones for earlier use.

In late summer direct sow Japanese onions for overwintering. Rake the soil to a fine texture and sow 1/2in. (1cm) deep. Thin to 4in. (10cm) apart each way. They will be ready before midsummer (when onions are expensive) but do not try to keep them after summer because they go off easily.

Pickling onions are sown thickly so that they crowd each other. 'Paris Silverskin' is the usual cultivar to choose, although pickling shallots are a good alternative to try.

Scallions should be sown 1/2in. (1cm) deep and 1/2in. (1cm) apart in early fall for spring use, and again in late winter and early spring for successional crops. The spring sowings can be grown with carrots as an intercrop.

If onion flies are a problem in your area grow sets, which rarely suffer from the pest, or grow under netting or floating row cover. If the leaves get a gray mold, dust them with wood ash, which will check the attack. If white rot or stem nematodes appear dig up and discard the affected plants (see page 42). Weed around onions by hand so that you do not damage or break the leaves or bulbs when you are cultivating soil close by.

There are many different onions available.
• 'Sturon' and 'Turbo' are excellent sets.
• 'Giant Zittau', 'Bedfordshire Champion', and 'Southport Red Globe' can be grown from seed.
• 'Senshyu Yellow' and 'Imai' are the best Japanese onions for overwintering.

## Brassicas

Brassicas can be started in small pots, but the most reliable crops are sown direct in a seedbed. When seedlings are about 3in. (8cm) high, lift them to break the taproot and replant in a seedbed, 3in. (8cm) apart. When they are about 6in. (15cm) high, transplant the seedlings. Make a deep hole at the recommended spacing for individual types. Add diluted seaweed solution and sifted compost, seaweed meal, and calcified seaweed. Plant seedlings to the depth of the lowest leaves and firm well.

All brassicas suffer from bird damage, so use black cotton. To prevent cabbage root fly attacks when they are transplanted, use 6in. (15cm) square pieces of old carpet, underlay, or roofing felt with a slit cut in one side. Push it around the stem of the seedling and lay it flat on the ground, to prevent the flies laying eggs in the soil.

Seedlings can also suffer from root flies in pots and seedbeds. Caterpillars can be hand-picked or sprayed with *Bacillus thuringiensis*, whiteflies can be controlled with soft soap if they start to increase, as can aphids. Keep the area wet to discourage flea beetles (see pages 38–43).

The worst problem suffered by brassicas is clubroot, which, once it gets into the soil is ineradicable. The best "cure" is prevention, so never buy in brassica plants. If you must, only buy ones grown in sterile potting mix, not soil. Wallflowers and stocks can carry the disease, and it may also be introduced with animal manure, which must always be thoroughly composted before use. Its virulence can be modified by heavily liming the soil before planting, and crops can be grown in pots, then transplanted to holes filled with sterile compost, so that infected soil does not touch your roots. Strict rotation of crops is essential where brassicas are concerned to prevent a buildup of the disease. Some new varieties are partly resistant.

### Broccoli

This overwintering crop is available in spring, when little else is growing. Sow in mid- to late spring in a seedbed and transplant, 30in. (75cm) apart each way, by midsummer.
• Try 'Early Purple', 'Late Purple', and 'White Sprouting' for succession.

### Broccoli raab

This fall broccoli is not winter hardy, and to do well it needs to be sown direct from mid- to late spring. With care, it can be started off in 3in. (8cm) pots if planted out 18in. (45cm) apart each way well before the root system fills the potting soil. It needs especially rich, moist soil. Mulch well with compost and water well in dry weather.
• 'Trixie', a new cultivar, is resistant to clubroot.
• 'Romanesco' has good texture and flavor but is more difficult to grow.

### Brussels sprouts

These can be available from midfall to early spring if several cultivars are grown. Sow successively from early to midspring and transplant to 2ft. (60cm) apart each way by midsummer in well-firmed soil. Plant them extra deep.
• 'Bedford Fillbasket' and 'Peer Gynt' are early.
• 'Icarus' gives a good late crop.

• 'Seven Hills' is recommended.
• 'Noisette' produces tiny, nutty sprouts.
• 'Rubine' has small, red sprouts.

### Cabbages

For early summer cabbages start in pots under glass from midwinter on, harden off in a cold frame and plant out, 18in. (45cm) apart each way, in early to midspring. To follow on, sow from late winter to early spring in the seedbed, planting out to 18in. (45cm) apart each way in late spring.

For early fall cabbages, sow in the seedbed in mid- to late spring and plant out, 18in. (45cm) apart each way, in early summer.

For late fall and early winter cabbages, sow in the seedbed in late spring to early summer and plant out, 2ft. (60cm) apart each way, in midsummer.

For spring cabbage, sow in mid- to late summer in the seedbed and plant out, 12in. (30cm) apart each way, in early to mid-fall.
• For early summer, plant 'Greyhound', 'Primo', or

*Below: A variety of broccoli raab called 'Mercedes'.*

*Above: The minicauliflower 'Garant' that grows particularly well on sandy soil.*

'Hispi', followed by 'Primo', or 'Grand Prize'.

• For early fall try 'Minicole', 'Winningstadt', and 'Red Drumhead'.

• For late fall and into winter sow 'Holland White', 'Celtic', 'Christmas Drumhead', and the crinkly leaved 'Savoy Ormskirk'.

• For spring sow 'Offenham' and 'Spring Hero'.

## Cauliflowers

Successive sowing of different cultivars will give cauliflowers almost year-round, but they are more difficult to grow than cabbages. They need very rich, moist soil, and their growth must not be checked at any stage or button-sized heads will result. Check that the level of lime is adequate, and keep the soil moist and well watered, especially in dry weather. Do not expect good results on light soils. When the curd starts to swell, bend the side leaves over to keep the light from yellowing it.

For summer and fall cauliflowers, sow in a seedbed in early to late spring and plant out, 2ft. (60cm) apart each way, from late spring to midsummer. For spring use, sow in mid- to late spring and plant out, 2ft. (60cm) apart each way, in early summer. On light soils and in small gardens use "minicaulis," which are close planted, 6in. (15cm) apart, and are best sown direct. They produce small heads, suitable for individual meals.

• For summer and fall cauliflowers sow 'All the Year Round', 'Mexico', and 'Snowcap'.

• For spring use sow 'Armado' and 'May Star'.

• 'Purple Cape' is red and reliable.

• The most reliable minicauli is 'Garant'.

## Chinese cabbage

Although this is grown alongside other brassicas, well-rotted manure or compost must be dug in beforehand. Sow direct, ½in. (1cm) deep and 12in. (30cm) apart, in rich, moist soil, or it will bolt, as will plants sown before midsummer. Sow successively from midsummer to early fall, protecting later sowings with a hoop house. Keep moist and well watered.

• 'Green Towers' is a bolt-resistant cultivar, which may do well from late spring.

*Below: Curly kale, seen here among the asparagus fern, is hardy and reliable.*

### Kale

This is the hardiest brassica of all. It is also nutritious, fairly resistant to clubroot and cabbage root flies, and is not usually eaten by birds. Sow in mid- to late spring, planting out 18in. (45cm) apart each way, in early summer.

• Grow 'Dark Green Curled' or 'Pentland Brig'.

*Above: Purple broccoli, one of the most reliable, nutritious, and hardy of spring crops.*

## Leaves

### Lettuces, endives, and chicory

Lettuces are one of the easiest crops to grow well and yet they are often badly grown. Never sow a lot of seed at once. They can be sown in situ, $^1\!/_2$in. (1cm) deep and 6–10in. (15–25cm) apart, or grown in a seedbed and planted out. Without doubt, the best way is to use multicelled packs.

Sow a few cells each of several types every few weeks through most of the year. Thin to one plant per cell and plant out as intercrops. The biggest problem is slow growth, which makes them bitter, so water thoroughly.

Loose-leaf varieties are not uprooted but eaten on a cut-and-come-again basis, so make the best use of the ground. Romaine lettuces are tall and need tying up to blanch them or they may be bitter. Overwintered lettuces need to be grown under cover, not so much for the warmth as for protection from the weather and hungry creatures. The popular radicchio, which is dark red, is sown $^1\!/_2$in. (1cm) deep or started in cells like lettuce and planted out 10in. (25cm) apart each way from late spring to midsummer.

Endives are grown like lettuces, but they must be blanched or they are too bitter. They can be cropped on the cut-and-come-again basis, so are economical on the ground. Sow from late spring to late summer, $^1\!/_2$in. (1cm) deep and 12in. (30cm) apart each way. Better still, start them off in cells like lettuces.

Chicory produces heads that are grown like lettuces; they may be solid like a romaine or round and looser. They can be left until late fall, when the roots are lifted and the foliage cut off and stored in a cool place. Then, when wanted, they are packed in sand in a warm, dark place where they start to produce solid shoots, called chicons, which are a superb addition to winter salads. If they are not lifted, chicory plants may overwinter and produce early leaves for cutting before they start to bolt.

Keep birds off the lettuce plants with black cotton and be sure to control slugs. There is a wide range of lettuces, so try many different ones

to see which you like best and grows well for you.
- 'Tom Thumb' is quick from early sowings.
- 'All the Year Round', 'Great Lakes', 'May King', 'Salad Bowl' (red and green), and 'Webb's Wonder' are good for summer use.
- 'Little Gem' and 'Lobjoits Green Cos' are good romaine lettuces.
- For overwintering try 'Kwiek' and 'Kellys' (under cover).
- Grow 'Rossa de Verona' raddichio for all purposes.
- For forcing, grow 'Brussels Witloef'.

### Spinach

Perpetual spinach, called leaf beet, is easier to grow and more nutritious than annual spinach, but if you want the latter sow at intervals from early spring to late summer. Sow thinly, 1in. (2.5cm) deep, and thin to 7in. (18cm) apart each way. It can also be started in cells or pots if planted out while still very small. It is worth feeding the soil beforehand with a handful of seaweed meal per square yard or a bucketful of sifted compost, because it needs rich conditions, or it will bolt. Water well to encourage growth and prevent bolting. It is one of the best crops to grow through a plastic sheet mulch because the mulch keeps the leaves away from the soil and aids growth.

For winter and early spring, perpetual spinach can be grown. Sow in the same way in late summer. Hoop houses will protect the plants but may encourage mildew.

New Zealand spinach is another nonspinach that is used and grown in the same way. It survives much better in hot, dry conditions and is more reluctant to bolt. It does need more space, and is better started in pots and planted out, 2ft.

(60cm) apart each way. Water well. Never allow plants to dry out or they will bolt.

Protect spinach plants from birds with black cotton and be sure to use slug traps.
- The best annual spinach cultivars are 'Monstrous Viroflay', 'Avanti', and 'Medania'.
- For perpetual spinach try 'Sigmaleaf', which is really a summer spinach, and 'Broad Leaf Prickly'.
- 'Bergola' can be sown under cover from fall to spring.

### Swiss chard

Chards are beet grown for their leaf stems instead of their roots, and they are treated in the same way. This is one of the most productive crops for small gardens and will carry on producing until hard winter frosts.

Sow 12in. (30cm) apart each way in midspring and make a second sowing in midsummer for winter use. Water well in dry weather.

Slugs are the only serious problem, but red-stemmed Swiss chard may also suffer from attacks of blackflies.
- Red-stemmed Swiss chard is brightly colored and is attractive in the ornamental garden.

# Pods and seeds

### Bush beans

Sow under hoop houses in midspring and in the open garden from late spring to midsummer. Sow 2in. (5cm) deep and 12in. (30cm) apart each way. Bush beans are susceptible to late frosts, cold winds, and slug and bird damage, and will benefit immensely from plastic soda bottle cloches. Mulch after sowing with grass clippings to preserve moisture. Water in dry weather.

Aphids and slugs can be troublesome.
- Highly recommended cultivars include 'Canadian Wonder', 'Radar', and 'Masai'.
- For drying as navy beans try 'Brown Dutch' (although any cultivar will do).
- There are some climbing forms, which grow like pole beans but have the finer texture and flavor of bush beans; try 'Blue Lake'.

### Corn

This is a luxury that really needs to be cooked within about 30 minutes of being picked or it is not sweet.

Small cardboard tubes are ideal for sowing under cover in midspring. Sow a second crop direct, 1in. (2.5cm) deep and 2ft. (60cm) apart each way, in late spring. For sowing from seedlings dig each planting deep and wide. Water with diluted seaweed solution and add sifted compost and seaweed meal. Take the seedlings that were grown under cover and plant in the holes, with more sifted compost. Firm well and add a soda bottle cloche for protection. When the plant is about 12in. (30cm) high remove the cloche. Add more sifted compost, hilling up around the plant to encourage rooting. Firm well and add a mulch of grass cuttings to reduce moisture loss.

When sowing in situ each site is dug and improved and the seed sown 4in. (10cm) deep but covered with only 1in. (2.5cm) of soil. Add a soda bottle cloche for protection. When the plant is about 12in. (30cm) high remove the cloche. Add more sifted compost, hilling up around the plant to encourage rooting. Firm well and add a mulch of grass cuttings to reduce moisture loss.

Corn is best grown in a block to ensure pollination, and I find that potatoes, squashes, or nasturtiums are a good intercrop, keeping the soil moist and providing the young shoots with extra shelter. Do not grow extra-sweet cultivars near ordinary ones, because they cross-pollinate and give poorer results. Water well when the cobs start to swell.

Grow several cultivars to give a succession.
- 'Kelvedon Glory', 'Northern Extra Sweet', 'Champ', and 'Butterscotch' are my favorites.

### Fava beans

These nutritious beans are easy to grow. Extra early crops of long-pod cultivars may be raised from sowings made in late fall in mild conditions. They do best on fertile, well-drained soil. Avoid cold, wet conditions for overwintering or seeds may rot. Sow 2–3in. (5–8cm) deep from late winter to midspring, 6in. (15cm) apart each way. Provide support as they develop.

*Below: The climbing bush bean 'Blue Lake' is especially convenient for small vegetable gardens.*

Fava beans can be affected by blackflies (see page 39), bean weevils (see page 43), and chocolate spot. Pinch out the growing and flowering tips once they start flowering to prevent blackfly attacks, or use soft soap later. Fava beans intercrop well with potatoes, and summer savory helps to discourage blackflies.

- 'Aquadulce Claudia' and 'Express' are early.
- 'The Sutton' is good for small gardens.

## Garden peas, snow peas, snap peas, and asparagus peas

Peas are more work than most vegetables, but they are so delicious fresh that they are worth the effort, and, as legumes, they enrich the soil for other crops. Peas are one of the few crops better grown in rows.

Grow short types; although they produce less, they do not need as much or as strong support, and they do not shade out other crops as much as taller ones. In dry conditions peas are quicker to germinate if they are soaked for an hour or so before sowing, and adding a dash of seaweed solution helps to disguise their smell from mice. As peas need support, grow them down the middle of a bed, and grow potatoes, brassicas, carrots, or corn on either side. For succession, peas can be sown from late winter to midsummer. They can even be sown in late fall for over-wintering, but these overwintered plants rarely do well. I have found that one good watering when the flowers are finishing will improve yields substantially.

Snow peas have edible pods, so podding is unnecessary when they are young and tender, but they are usually tall and rapidly get tough. Snap peas are similar but have thicker, sweeter, edible pods. They also tend to be tall, except for 'Sugar Rae'. Asparagus peas are more like a vetch than peas. The pods can be eaten when they are small and tender. They grow in poor conditions and have pretty flowers.

Use pea guards to keep birds from eating the seeds and young leaves; if mice are a problem put down traps. Do not worry about mildew as it rarely affects yields.

- The round-seeded cultivars are the hardiest, but they are not as sweet; 'Meteor' is probably the best cultivar.
- The wrinkled-seeded cultivars are sweeter, so for later sowing grow 'Early Onward', 'Greenshaft', 'Kelvedon Wonder', and 'Rondo'.
- Petits pois are just small, sweet, wrinkle-seeded peas; grow 'Lynx' or 'Waverex'.

## Pole beans

This is an easy crop to grow, and cultivars with colored flowers and purple beans look attractive in ornamental areas. They are highly productive, but have a coarser texture and flavor than bush beans.

If your soil is very poor it will be worth improving conditions by digging in well-rotted compost before planting. Generally, however, these beans give a good crop without any special preparation. Seeds can be started off under cover in early spring, one seed per pot. Plant out in late spring after hardening off. Otherwise, sow in late spring, 2in. (5cm) deep and 9in. (23cm) apart. They need to be well mulched, watered, and picked regularly to do well.

Pole beans need to be supported on poles, wires, or strings, but netting is better and wire netting is best of all. All the supports can be suspended from posts, walls, or fences. Try growing the shorter varieties up and over corn if this has been started earlier in pots and planted out. Pinch out the plants when they reach the tops of the supports to encourage bushy growth.

Pole beans may suffer from slugs and aphids when they are small.

• Among the available cultivars try 'Desirée', 'Kelvedon Marvel', 'Scarlet Emperor', or 'Butler'.

### Okra

This is difficult to grow unless permanently heated conditions are available or unless it is grown in warm, sheltered areas with long, hot summers. Treat as eggplants (see page 104), but space 2ft. (60cm) apart. Support with canes and pinch out tips when plants are 12in. (30cm) high to encourage bushy growth.

Red spider mites, aphids, and whiteflies can be troublesome (see pages 38–43).

## Shoots and buds

### Asparagus

A real luxury, which takes three years before it becomes productive, but highly recommended if you have space. It has attractive foliage, so can be used in ornamental areas. It does best in a permanent bed on its own, as it takes a lot of space to yield any quantity. It can be grown under fruit (especially grapes) to save space.

Plant one-year-old crowns in early spring. Prepare a trench 10in. (25cm) deep and work in plenty of well-rotted manure or compost. Soak the crowns in water for an hour, then plant in the trench 6in. (15cm) deep and 2ft. (60cm) apart.

Asparagus is rarely affected by pests and diseases so no special treatment is required.

• New hybrids are appearing that are all male and do not waste energy producing seed; otherwise, there is little to choose from between cultivars.

### Celery and celeriac

These need careful tending and permanently moist, rich soil to grow well. They are not easy. If you want celery just for the flavor, grow it like parsley, let it self-sow, and use the leaves.

Celery needs to be surface-sown in tiny pots or cells in a propagating unit, in late winter or early spring. The seed is difficult to sow individually, so thin early and pot up into 2–3in. (5–8cm) pots. Harden off in a cold frame and plant in late spring. Plant out 12in. (30cm) apart in trenches filled with well-rotted compost or manure. Protect with plastic soda bottles or hoop houses. Water thoroughly and make sure that the plants never dry out. Once they are about three-quarters grown, surround each one with a collar of newspaper and hill up to blanch them. Continue hilling up every three weeks as the plants grow.

Celeriac is started in the same way as celery and requires the same moist, rich soil. It is, however, more forgiving. No trenches are needed, but well-rotted manure should be dug in in winter. Plant out 12in. (30cm) apart and keep well watered. It can be persuaded to produce a swollen root by most gardeners, and no blanching is needed. Strip off lower leaves as the root starts to swell.

It is essential to take precautions against slugs. Celery flies and carrot rust flies may also attack plants (see page 39).

• Two popular celery cultivars are 'Giant Pink' and 'Giant Red'.

• Celeriac is becoming widely available; look for the variety 'Monarch'.

## Fennel

Grown for its bulblike leaf bases, which have an aniseed flavor, fennel is native to Mediterranean regions but it can be grown in more temperate areas provided it has a sunny site and moist, rich soil.

It is best sown in late spring to late summer, either in the open or in cells sown in the greenhouse, and planted out when small at 12in. (30cm) apart each way. Keep watered at all times; do not let plants dry out or they will bolt and run to seed. Hill up the bases when they begin to swell and continue hilling up for 3–4 weeks. Slugs may be a problem.

## Globe artichoke

Artichokes are attractive plants, which can be used in ornamental areas, but they do better given their own bed of rich soil. Rotate every third year or so. Purple artichokes taste better than the green ones but have small thorns on the buds.

Sow in pots in midspring and plant out seedlings the following summer, 3ft. (1m) apart each way. They are also grown by planting suckers, with roots attached, taken from mature plants. They are easy to grow but may be lost in hard, wet winters unless protected with straw or hoop houses. Water well in dry weather.

Globe artichokes are rarely badly affected by pests and diseases.

## Sea kale

This is rarely grown, although it produces a tasty, nutritious crop and is attractive enough to be grown in ornamental areas.

Sea kale needs a rich soil; dig in plenty of well-rotted manure or compost before planting. Sow in a seedbed and grow for a year, then

*Above: A ready-to-pick globe artichoke head makes a delicious treat for midsummer.*

*Above: When sea kale stalks appear, cut the head off at ground level. The crown will crop for many years.*

transplant to a permanent position in late winter. Plant out in an open, sunny position, allowing 18in. (45cm) each way, and grow on until fall. They are easier to grow from "thongs" or crowns (if available). Do not crop for two years after planting. To crop, put bottomless buckets over the crowns in dry weather in winter and cover to a depth of 9in. (23cm) with a mixture of peat substitute or leafmold and sand.

Sea kale is usually trouble free, although slugs may be a problem.

• The cultivar 'Lily White' is still available.

# Fruits

### Cucumbers

These need continuous warmth and moisture under cover, with a really rich soil for the best varieties, although there are inferior forms that will crop in cold frames or even out of doors in good seasons.

Greenhouse cucumbers need to be sown in pots in a heated propagating unit in late winter to early spring. They are then potted up until planted out in mid- to late spring. They must have continuous high temperatures of 70–75°F (21–24°C) and very high humidity. If the greenhouse is unheated, do not plant out until late spring. Plant in border soil or plant individually in 12in. (30cm) pots. Support the plants by tying to bamboo canes or twisting them gently around strings attached to the roof. Pinch out the growing point when the plant reaches the roof and regularly trim sideshoots back to two leaves.

Any male flowers on cucumbers must be removed (there is no tiny cucumber behind them) before they open so that the females are not pollinated, or bitter fruit will result. Keep well

*Left: A tender eggplant ready for picking. Fruits should be harvested before the seeds form and any surplus can be frozen, either sliced or as ratatouille.*

*Above: Pick zucchini regularly to encourage further fruiting—any that are left grow on.*

*Above: The pumpkin variety 'Golden Nugget' has an excellent flavor combined with a compact habit.*

watered and spray plants and paths with water to keep humidity high. Give a liquid feed regularly to promote growth. In very warm sites or with electric heating they can be planted in cold frames, but they are not easy to grow well.

• New varieties such as 'Aidas', 'Carmen', 'Fembaby', and 'Petita' are easy.

Ridge or outdoor cucumbers and pickling cucumbers are of lower quality and often have little prickles. They benefit from a cold frame or cloches, and are often better grown in a cold greenhouse or hoop house. Dig in well-rotted manure or compost before sowing. Sow in pots in a propagating unit in midspring, keep warm, and pot up until planted out, 2ft. (60cm) apart each way, under cover in late spring. Alternatively, sow under hoop houses in late spring to early summer. Do not remove male flowers. They trail like squashes so can also be grown up fences or over a trellis once they are vigorous enough to fill the cloche or cold frame. Syringe regularly and mulch to conserve moisture. Give a liquid feed regularly.

• The Japanese cultivar 'Kyoto' is excellent.

• 'Marketmore' is worth trying.

Cucumbers are prone to spider mites (see page 42) and mildew (see page 47).

## Eggplants

These are definitely a greenhouse crop and need continuous warm, moist conditions. Sow in pots in a propagating unit or on a sunny windowsill in early spring. Repot each month, then plant under cover in midspring in a heated greenhouse or late spring in an unheated greenhouse. Plant in border soil 18in. (45cm) apart and support with canes. Water and liquid feed regularly. Allow 5–6 fruits a plant and pinch out tops when 12in. (30cm) high.

Eggplants are susceptible to spider mites and aphids, so need regular spraying with soft soap (see page 31) or the use of biological controls (see page 33).

• There are several cultivars; try 'Long Purple'.

## Peppers

These need warm, moist conditions, preferably in a greenhouse, although they do often succeed planted out or grown in large pots against a warm wall. Sow in pots in a propagating unit or on a warm windowsill in late winter to early spring. Repot monthly, then plant under cover in mid- to late spring; if it is cold plant only in a heated greenhouse. Use 12in. (30cm) pots and support with canes. Pinch out the growing tip when plants are 6in. (15cm) tall. Water regularly and foliar feed with dilute seaweed solution.

Chili peppers can be very hot, despite growing in the cool, and are prolific.

They need spraying with soft soap against aphids. Keep an eye out for slug damage to ripening fruit. Interplant with basil, which likes

the same conditions.
- For enormous sweet peppers grow 'Big Bertha'.
- 'Californian Wonder' and 'Canape' are also good.

### Summer and winter squashes

These closely related plants need a very rich, well-manured soil to do well. They will flourish on the compost pile.

Sow in pots in the warm in midspring and plant out, 3ft. (90cm) apart each way, in late spring once the last frost has gone. They can also be sown direct under a hoop house or plastic soda bottles in late spring. Most varieties of summer squash produce long stems, which can be trained up fences or along wires. They can be grown under and over corn, if it is well established, or wound around sunflower stems. Keep well watered, especially in dry weather, and give a liquid feed when the fruits begin to appear. As they grow large, squashes and pumpkins should be propped up on bricks or pieces of wood to keep them off the soil and to prevent them from rotting. It is not worth saving the seed because plants cross-pollinate freely.

Watch out for slug damage, but otherwise squashes have few problems.
- Among the available zucchini look out for 'All Green Bush', and 'Ambassador'.
- 'Golden Zucchini' has yellow fruit.
- 'Long Green Trailing' is probably the best summer squash, and 'Green Bush' is a compact form, more like a zucchini plant.
- 'Custard White' ('Patty Pan') has round, flat fruit on compact plants.
- 'Golden Nugget' is the best and tastiest of the pumpkins, with a compact habit.
- 'Uchiki Kuri' is a similar Japanese form and has sweeter, nutty fruits.
- 'Mammoth' grows large, takes even more space, and has little culinary value.

### Tomatoes

These need well-enriched soil. Sow in pots in a propagating unit in late winter and early spring for indoor crops and in midspring for outdoor crops. Pot up twice and keep warm until hardened off. Plant out, at 2ft. (60cm) apart each way, in midspring under cover or in late spring to early summer outdoors.

*Below: A large, succulent green pepper bears fruit in a warm greenhouse.*

Most cultivars are normally grown as single cordons tied to canes, with all the sideshoots rubbed off. I sometimes grow plants as double and triple cordons, because these give bigger, earlier crops. Sideshoots that are removed early on can be potted up, and they will easily root to make new plants. Indeterminate types or non-deshooted plants produce many sprawling stems, and to keep these and the fruit off the soil I place old wire baskets over the young plants, which grow up through them. These can also be covered with a plastic sheet to act as cloches while the plants establish. Outdoors they always benefit from cloches or at least wind protection with nets on stakes, and these can be used later to protect the plants from birds.

Growing under cover gives bigger yields, which come earlier. Plant the tomatoes directly into the soil in the greenhouse or hoop house rather than using pots. The extra watering and feeding can never replace a free root-run. The soil will become tired if tomatoes are grown in it year after year, so dig it out and refill with enriched, fresh topsoil every few years or so.

Feeding is not really necessary in rich, loamy soil, but it is needed by plants in poor soil or containers. Comfrey liquid (see page 16) is ideal for feeding tomatoes. For early crops be careful not to overfeed, because this produces growth instead of fruit. I find that the fruit from underfed plants tastes better, although starved ones just do badly. Do not overfeed even maincrops. Water well but not too often if plants are in the ground, without allowing them to be checked, which causes blossom end rot or splitting. In pots or containers it is harder to get an even water balance. Water tomato plants frequently and keep

*Above: There is a tremendous range of tomato varieties, so grow several for different flavors. These 'Marmande' tomatoes are tasty and good for salads.*

the medium constantly moist once vigorous growth starts. Tomatoes ripen best on the plant. Leave a ripe one or a banana in the greenhouse to help others to ripen.

Tomato crops rarely suffer badly from pests and diseases, especially if they are grown with French marigolds and basil. Soft soap and predators (see pages 31 and 33) will deal with whitefly infestations in the greenhouse.

Grow several different tomato cultivars for different flavors and uses.
• 'Pink Brandywine' tastes best of all but has poor disease resistance.
• 'Gardener's Delight' tastes very good.
• 'Marmande' and 'Dombito' beefsteaks produce large, tasty tomatoes, but to get really big ones limit the number of fruits to three or four to a plant at a time.
• 'San Marzano' and plum-type ones taste poor raw but are wonderful cooked.
• 'Moravi' and 'Aromata' are most reliable greenhouse varieties.

# The fruit garden

Growing organic fruit is easier and makes more sense than growing vegetables. Shop-bought fruit is never really fresh, and the plants grown are chosen for their high yield, rather than for their flavor. At home you can choose old-fashioned cultivars with good flavor and high vitamin content.

flowering period. A crabapple will pollinate most others that are also in flower.

Apples suffer infestations of several pests and diseases, such as woolly aphids, codling moths, apple sawflies, wasps, canker, scab, and rot, but as long as damaged fruits are removed during successive thinnings there should still be plenty of fruit. Apply sticky bands in early fall and check them throughout winter to catch most winter moths. Use pheromone traps to prevent codling moth maggots attacking valuable crops. Scabby patches on fruit are related to blisters and blotches on twigs and leaves, so prune these out and allow more air and light into the tree, and then mulch and feed to stimulate growth and

## Tree fruit

### Apples

Apple trees are not fussy about soil or site, although very wet sites may encourage scab and canker, and they prefer a slightly acidic soil. Most apples can be grown as cordons, 2ft. (60cm) apart, and as espaliers, at about 10ft. (3m) apart, to give high-quality fruit and to squeeze in as many cultivars as possible in a small space. They can also be grown as fans, stepovers, and festoons. Some, known as tip-bearers, such as 'Beauty of Bath' and 'George Cave', are better grown as rarely pruned dwarf bushes. If you are planning to grow apples in containers, make sure you use a semi-dwarfing rootstock.

Pollinating partners are best provided by growing several different cultivars that share a

*Below: Any apples which are not quite up to standard for eating can be made into delicious apple juice.*

spray once a month with seaweed solution. This will also discourage canker "ulcers," which often occur on poor growers. Brown, rotten patches on apples are caused by bruising or damage and then infection by spores overwintering in stems and soil. Mulching and seaweed sprays will encourage healthy growth. Small trees and bushes should be netted against birds.

• Among early croppers are 'George Cave' and 'Discovery'.

• Good late keepers include 'Ashmead's Kernel', 'Winston', 'Wagener', and 'Tydeman's Late Orange'.

• Outstanding midseason apples include 'James Grieve', 'Orleans Reinette', and 'Charles Ross'.

• 'Bramley' is a good cooker, but 'Reverend W. Wilks' and 'Howgate Wonder' are also good.

• Some of the new cultivars are worth considering, including 'Greensleeves', "Jonagold', 'Jupiter', 'Katja', and 'Spartan'.

• Even 'Golden Delicious' tastes good when it is grown organically at home.

## Peaches, nectarines, and almonds

These three plants have the same cultivation needs, and are ideal additions to the ornamental garden. Grown as bushes, about 15ft. (4.5m) apart, peaches are easy, self-fertile, and fruitful as long as they have rich, moist soil and are kept well mulched. They all do better in the sunnier drier regions, or in a greenhouse when they're best grown in containers and hand-pollinated. Nectarines will not crop as bushes and need the warmth of a sunny wall or greenhouse, but almonds can be grown as bushes or trees and do not require thinning or pruning.

Trees must be sprayed with Bordeaux mixture just before leaf-fall and again in late winter to early spring to prevent peach leaf curl, which

*Above: 'Rochester' peaches are highly recommended grown as bushes, or even as specimen trees, where their beauty can be seen.*

puckers and discolors the leaves and weakens the tree. The disease can be avoided if the trees are overwintered indoors or if a plastic sheet is hung over them. The sheet can be hung from the top of the wall over a fan-trained tree to keep the branches dry throughout winter and to late spring, and it will also provide protection from frost. Frosts will take off the blossoms and fruitlets in most years in temperate areas, so they must be covered on cold nights. On plants grown against walls and under cover, spider mites can be a problem; spray frequently with water and introduce *Phytoseiulus persimilis* (predatory mite). Plants in the greenhouse can also be affected by mildew and scale insects (see pages 42 and 47).

• Among the best peaches for growing as bushes or standard trees are 'Peregrine' and 'Rochester'.

## Pears

Late frosts can damage blossom, and pears are usually best grown as fans or espaliers against a sunny wall. Because they are large trees, pears are usually grown on quince rootstocks, to give small to medium trees. Pollinating partners are needed, and even partially self-fertile cultivars ('Conference', 'Docteur Jules Guyot', and 'Durondeau') give better fruits if pollinated. Pears need a fairly rich soil and suffer badly from grass competition, so clear the ground of all perennial weeds before planting.

Leaf blackening in spring is usually caused by harsh winds, but fireblight might cause the flowers and leaves to wither and brown. Prune out and burn affected shoots before the problem spreads. Leaf blistering is caused by mites; spray with soft soap. Fruits sometimes blacken and drop with pear midge maggots inside; collect these up and destroy them. Pears also suffer from winter moth, woolly aphids, codling moth, sawfly, canker, scab, and brown rot, and birds and wasps can often be troublesome.

- 'Doyenné du Comice' (late fall) is outstanding, but it needs a wall; it's pollinated by 'Beurré Hardy', 'Docteur Jules Guyot', or 'Glou Morceau'.
- Pears good as bushes include 'Beurré Hardy' (midfall), 'Williams Bon Chrétien' (early fall), 'Clapp's Favourite' (late summer), and 'Jargonelle' (late summer).
- 'Glou Morceau' is probably the best-flavored keeper.
- 'Docteur Jules Guyot' (early fall) and 'Conference' (midfall) are ideal for a two-pear garden.
- 'Beth' (early fall) is a compact form.
- Asian, Nashi, pears are self-fertile and trouble-free; try 'Kumoi' or 'Shinseiki'.

## Plums and damsons

Although these can be grown on dwarfing rootstock and trained, they're better grown as bushes or semi-dwarfs. They like richer conditions than apples or

*Below: Purple 'Pershore' plums for conserves.*

pears, and near the compost pile is ideal. Both damsons and European plums are self-fertile, but most plums need pollination partners.

Plums suffer from several pests and diseases, including rust, bacterial canker, silverleaf, plum sawflies, spider mites, and, especially, woolly aphids, although most do not affect the crops (see pages 38–49). Birds and wasps destroy most plums, and birds also take off buds in winter. Use black cotton after leaf-fall and, if possible, net to protect the fruit. Fruit moth maggots can be prevented with pheromone traps, and earwigs can be stopped by sticky bands. Gummosis may cause oozing from the bark on badly drained or acidic soil. Prune only in summer to avoid silverleaf.

• It is hard to beat 'Victoria' (early fall), even though it is susceptible to disease.
• 'Coe's Golden Drop' (early fall) is tasty but shy to fruit.
• 'Reine Claude de Bavais' (early fall) is a good cropper.
• 'Oullin's Gage' (late summer) and 'Marjorie's Seedling' (early fall) are good for frosty areas.

# Soft fruit

### Blackberries and hybrid berries
Grow in rich, moist conditions, although they will fruit in poor soil and even in moderate shade. After planting, cut down each cane to a bud about 12in. (30cm) above ground level, and because they fruit on one-year-old wood it is important to keep the old and new canes separate. Cut out old canes after fruiting.

Boysenberries (midsummer) are large and well flavored but do not crop heavily, and the loganberry LY654 is productive and flavorsome. Tayberry has large, sweet fruits and does better in light shade than in full sun.

Despite potential problems including aphids, virus diseases, raspberry beetles, cane spot, spur blight, and botrytis (see pages 38–49) these plants tend to crop heavily.
• Among the many cultivars 'Himalayan Giant' is the biggest and toughest (grow it as a boundary or trained over a fence to keep it upright); it is productive from early fall and does not need a lot of space to do well.
• 'Bedford Giant' fruits in late summer.
• 'Oregon Cutleaf' is thornless but too late (midfall) for cold areas.

### Blackcurrants
These are self-fertile plants, but it is worth having several cultivars to spread the flowering and later cropping. They need rich, moist, heavy soil and must be planted deep and grown as a stool,

*Below: Blackcurrants are a rich source of vitamin C.*

because they fruit best on young wood. Prune in late summer by cutting out all fruited wood.

Net plants to protect from birds. Aphids can curl leaf tips in early summer; dip them in a bucket of soft soap solution. Big bud is a common problem, but in midwinter pick off the bigger, rounded buds and discard them. Reversion, a virus infection, is spread by big bud. Plants are also susceptible to mildew and leaf spot (see pages 38–49). If yields drop and do not improve with feeding, grub up the bushes and plant new ones.

• Some mildew-resistant forms are available, including 'Ben Lomond', 'Ben Sarek', and 'Ben More' (all midsummer).

• 'Mendip Cross' is a good early cropper.

• 'Westwick Choice' is late.

• 'Wellington XXX' (midsummer) is also recommended.

### Gooseberries

Bushes need moisture and a rich soil, but will tolerate some shade; avoid planting in hot, dry spots. Prune after fruiting to give an erect, open-centered bush.

Mildew is a problem in dry conditions, and it spreads from the tips to the berries; keep plants well watered and mulched. Birds are the main pest, eating not only the fruit in summer but also the buds in winter; leave pruning until early spring, and then wind black cotton around the bush. The gooseberry sawfly caterpillar will defoliate young bushes; put a sheet underneath the bush and shake it: the caterpillars can be picked up as they fall.

• Among the best cultivars are 'Leveller' (large green), 'Early Sulphur' (early yellow), and 'Langley Gage' (white sweet).

• If there is space for only one, grow the mildew-

*Above: Gooseberries are available in widely varying flavors and can be deliciously sweet even when raw. The 'Keepsake' variety is particularly delicious.*

resistant and reliable 'Invicta' variety.

• 'Rokula' and 'Greenfinch' are also both good gooseberries which are resistant to mildew.

• 'Keepsake' is a delicious variety.

### Raspberries

Plant in a sheltered spot in full sun, if possible, although they will tolerate some shade. They need rich, moist soil and mulching to do really well, and add well-rotted manure or compost in the bottom of the planting trench. Mulch well in spring and water regularly in dry weather. Buy in new stock every ten years or so.

Birds are a problem, and raspberries must be netted or caged. Fall-fruiting forms rarely suffer from maggots; but for summer fruiters rake over the mulch in winter to expose overwintering larvae to the birds. Despite raspberry beetle, cane spot, cane blight, spur blight, cane midges, wasps, and various viral diseases, raspberries tend to crop heavily if new stock is bought every few years.

• 'Glen Ample', 'Glen Moy', 'Glen Magna', and 'Autumn Bliss' are good, but visit a pick-your-own outlet to try other cultivars before choosing.

## Redcurrants and whitecurrants

These prefer a lighter soil than blackcurrants and will tolerate light shade. Mulch in spring and spray with liquid seaweed.

Plants must be netted to stop birds taking the fruit. They are susceptible to leaf blistering aphids, which pucker and discolor the leaves but do not affect the yields; they are cleared away with summer pruning. They may suffer from aphids, sawfly, and leaf spot (see pages 38–49) but are usually trouble free.

• There is little to choose among the different available cultivars, although 'Four Lands' is an early redcurrant.

## Strawberries

Plant in late summer in humus-rich, thoroughly weeded soil. For consistent cropping, replace about a third of the plants every year, because fewer and smaller fruits are borne by three-year-old plants. Buy completely new stock every five years or so.

New cultivars are more likely to be resistant to attacks of mold.

• Fall-fruiting forms such as 'Mara des Bois' are not as sweet (they have less sun) but are still worth growing.

• 'Aromel' will fruit in fall if the first flower trusses are removed.

• 'Honeoye' and 'Marshmello' are tasty.

• 'Royal Sovereign' is excellent but difficult to find.

*Above: As raspberries vary in flavor go to a pick-your-own farm and try several before choosing. Try yellow raspberries which are exceptional.*

*Below: Redcurrants have quite a sharp flavor raw, but they reward well when cooked with other fruits and make delicious conserves.*

# Herbs

Herbs are an essential part of any garden, being both decorative and useful. Traditionally, they have been cultivated for their culinary and medicinal properties, although some have other uses, providing scents, fibers, dyes, or cosmetics. They are particularly suited to the organic garden as they are virtually invulnerable to pests and diseases, and their scented flowers attract bees and other beneficial insects.

Herbs are ideal plants to grow if space is limited. With only a tiny area to cultivate it makes sense to grow small, quick-growing herbs for adding to salads and in cooking. You can even grow a few in windowboxes, pots, or containers.

Many perennial herbs (see pages 116–19) are useful as companion plants, and in a large garden they can be grown in a variety of different places and picked systematically. Perennial herbs are especially good companions for fruit trees and bushes, and as borders or hedges around other areas, especially vegetable beds. Ornamental areas can consist solely of perennial herbs, which are productive yet need little maintenance. Aromatic perennials thrive close to walls and pathways and to ornaments made of brick and stone, which retain the warmth that these plants love. Many attractive herb gardens are designed with a formal arrangement of brick or stone pathways radiating from a central ornament or birdbath.

If space is limited, most perennial herbs can be grown in pots or containers, but do not expect them to flourish as vigorously as they would in the ground. Of course, in pots they can be stood under cover, in a cold frame or greenhouse, to extend their season. Do not take them into centrally heated rooms, however, as they will not do well. Container growing is ideal for mints, which are invasive and not easy to control when grown in a bed with other plants as they soon take over all the available space.

## Annual herbs

Most annual herbs are best sown direct in their final position in midspring. They resent transplanting and will not make as much growth if started in small pots or cells. Mark out and spot sow as for vegetables; most annual herbs do not need sowing or thinning to one plant per site. Alternatively, sow in small pots, pot up if necessary, then harden off and plant out after the last frost.

**Arugula** (*Eruca vesicaria* subsp. *sativa*)
Arugula, which gets to 2ft. (60cm), is easy to grow but tastes best when grown quickly in moist conditions. Sow in pots or directly in the soil 6in.

*Above: Borage is grown for its pretty blue flowers.*

*Above: Coriander is a valuable cooking ingredient.*

(15cm) apart from early spring to early fall. It is susceptible to flea beetles.

### Basil (*Ocimum basilicum*)

One of the best-flavored herbs, basil grows between 6 and 24in. (15 and 60cm) tall. There are purple-leaved, tiny-leaved, and lemon-flavored forms as well as the usual sweet basil. Start off in pots in the warm and plant out 8in. (20cm) apart each way when all danger of frost is passed. Basil likes a warm, sheltered position, so grow alongside tomatoes or peppers, which like similar conditions. Watch out for aphids and cut the plants back before flowering.

### Borage (*Borago officinalis*)

Borage, which gets to 2–3ft. (60–90cm), tends to sprawl so is best at the back of borders. Sow in position, thin to 18in. (45cm) apart and allow to self-seed thereafter. With occasional trimming, the plants can be in flower most of late spring and summer. The blue flowers are attractive to bees.

### Caraway (*Carum carvi*)

Grow caraway, which will get to 2ft. (60cm), in a sunny site and rich soil. Sow in position and thin to 8in. (20cm) apart in spring or fall. If left to flower in the second year it may self-seed.

### Chervil (*Anthriscus cerefolium*)

This herb, growing to 12in. (30cm), is like parsley but is easier to grow and has a milder flavor. Sow chervil from early spring to late summer in partial shade in a light, well-drained soil and thin to 6in. (15cm) apart. Chervil will self-seed if left to flower, and if plants are cut down before flowering they will produce new crops of fresh foliage.

### Coriander (*Coriandrum sativum*)

Plants grow to 1–2ft. (30–60cm) tall. Sow in position about 10in. (25cm) apart in late spring, choosing a site with full sun and rich soil.

### Cumin (*Cuminum cyminum*)

A short plant, 6–12in. (15–30cm) tall, cumin needs a warm, sheltered site and a well-drained soil. Spot sow in early summer at 2in. (5cm) apart. Support the plants with sticks to stop seedheads falling over and getting dirty.

*Above: Curled parsley is milder than flat-leaved.*

*Above: Pick summer savory as its flower buds form.*

**Dill** (*Anethum graveolens*)
Dill plants grow to 3ft. (90cm) tall. Sow seeds direct or in pots and plant them out 12in. (30cm) apart in full sun and a rich soil. If they are left to flower, dill attracts flower flies.

**Europe sage** (*Salvia sclarea*)
This handsome and stately herb, which grows to 2–3ft. (60–90cm) in height, is a member of the sage family; its lilac flowers are showy and are attractive to bees. Sow the seeds in pots and plant out 12in. (30cm) apart. Pick the leaves before flowers appear.

**Marigold** (*Calendula officinalis*)
Pot marigolds grow to 2ft. (60cm). Sow in pots or direct in position 12in. (30cm) apart from early spring to early fall, and allow to self-seed.

**Parsley** (*Petroselinum crispum*)
Parsley grows to about 12in. (30cm). The bigger, plain-leaved variety (*P. crispum* 'Italian') has more flavor than the curly-leaved form.

Parsley is biennial, so flowers in the second year after sowing; leave to seed because self-sown plants are always best. Sow soaked seed on the soil surface and barely cover the seed. The seeds can take a long time to germinate. Sow once in spring and again in fall for two years running, then use the self-sown seedlings that appear. Thin plants to 6in. (15cm) apart. Parsley revels in rich moist conditions and can stand moderate shade.

**Summer savory** (*Satureja hortensis*)
Plants grow to 18in. (45cm). Sow shallowly in pots or direct at 6in. (15cm) apart. It can be dug up and potted to put under cover for winter use.

# Perennial herbs

Most perennial herbs will tolerate drier, poorer soils than annual herbs. Many are native to the Mediterranean region and need sunshine and a light well-drained soil to do well. It is the combination of damp and cold that kills them, and they may need some shelter or a hoop house to come through bad winters—growing them against a wall is often sufficient help. In well-sheltered or urban gardens most perennial herbs will last for many years.

Almost all are good at suppressing weeds, suffer from few pests and diseases, and need little maintenance apart from cutting back dead, overgrown, and excessive growth.

Most are best bought as young plants rather than grown from seed. Many are easily grown from cuttings or dividing existing plants, so visit your friends' gardens with something to trade. Do not divide or move herbs in fall or winter, and plant up a new herb bed in spring. Cutting back most herbs each spring removes withered growths and produces a flush of new shoots. Leave pruning until spring so that the old growth protects the new against bad weather. Take care not to cut back too far, or the plant may die; go no further than where live green shoots emerge from the older wood.

### Anise (*Myrrhis odorata*)
Plants grow to 3ft. (1m) tall. Sow in fall in light shade and transplant 2ft. (60cm) apart in spring. The plant's fernlike leaves are decorative.

### Chives (*Allium schoenoprasum*)
Chives, which grow to 12in. (30cm) in height, can be started from seed or separated from existing clumps, which anyhow will benefit from being divided every other year. Plant them as neat and effective border edgings and remove the flowering heads from alternate plants to get both flowers and foliage. Grow under fruit trees and roses for their companion effects: the flowers attract beneficial insects, especially bees.

### Common balm (*Melissa officinalis*)
This plant, which grows to 2ft. (60cm), resembles a mint but does not have the tendency to spread. Compact and dense, it excludes weeds when planted 18in. (45cm) apart and will flourish almost anywhere. There is a yellow variegated form, which is especially valuable in ornamental areas.

### Feverfew (*Tanacetum parthenium*)
This short-lived perennial, to 18in. (45cm), self-seeds with a vengeance. It is a good foil for other plants and is an excellent companion plant, discouraging pests, making it especially worth growing as a space filler.

### Garden lovage (*Levisticum officinale*)
Garden lovage is a herbaceous plant, to 6ft. (2m), which grows best in moist, shady spots. Propagate by root division or seed. The flowerheads attract flower flies.

### Horseradish (*Armoracia rusticana*)
Horseradish will grow to 2ft. (60cm). It is usually started from plant cuttings and needs well-cultivated soil because the roots go deep. Plant at the bottom of the garden or in an out-of-the-way spot, as it spreads by the roots and is hard to eradicate once established.

### Lavender (*Lavandula* spp.)
The gorgeously perfumed shrub, 1–3ft. (30–90cm), will attract bees and butterflies. There are many forms, in a range of sizes and flower colors. Plant in well-drained soil in a sunny position.

### Lemon beebrush (*Aloysia triphylla*)
The shrub, which grows to 3ft. (90cm), has an exquisite lemon sherbet scent, which the dried leaves retain for many months. Easily grown from cuttings, it is not hardy and gets killed above ground by hard frosts. Plant 3ft. (90cm) apart

*Above: Lavender is both decorative and fragrant.*

*Above: The showy leaves of variegated common balm.*

against a warm wall and protect the roots from damp and cold; they sprout like fuchsias in spring. It can be kept in a pot and overwintered under cover or as a houseplant but is then susceptible to aphids and spider mites.

### Marjoram (*Origanum*)

There are several varieties, all of which are similar to oregano and grow to about 12in. (30cm). All prefer a sunny position. Propagate by seed for the best-flavored ones, which are grown as annuals except in warm climates, and by root division for the tougher perennials. These latter tend to form low mounds, which make them useful as informal edging or to go under fruit trees and bushes. There is an attractive golden form that turns a butter-cream yellow in summer and reverts to green in winter. In flower, marjorams attract bees and butterflies.

### Mint (*Mentha* spp.)

There are many species and forms of mint, which grow to 18–36in. (45–90cm). They are invasive. Never put mints in with other herbs as the roots penetrate everything. Grow them in pots, containers almost submerged in the soil, or in

beds surrounded by concrete or regularly cut grass. Cool, refreshingly scented forms, such as peppermint (*M. x piperita*) and spearmint (*M. spicata*), suit ornamental areas, as do golden and silver variegated, yellow, gray, and curly forms, which are mostly less vigorous. Mints make cheap and effective, low-maintenance groundcover for large areas, especially under trees, and they encourage bees and beneficial insects.

### Rosemary (*Rosmarinus officinalis*)

Rosemary, which grows to 2ft. (60cm), is not hardy but usually survives in colder climates if given a warm spot against a wall and well-drained soil. It makes a good hedging plant if kept well trimmed, otherwise it tends to sprawl. It will also grow in a pot under cover. It is easily propagated from cuttings in spring The flowers are loved by bees.

### Sage (*Salvia*)

Easily grown from cuttings or seed and getting to 2ft. (60cm), sage needs replacing every few years as it becomes straggly and resents pruning. The red form has a fine flavor; the more compact, multi-colored sages are not hardy.

*Above: Rosemary can be picked all year round.*

*Above: Red sage is a beautiful and aromatic plant.*

### Scarlet beebalm (*Monarda didyma*)

A herbaceous plant, to 3ft. (90cm), with beautiful scarlet flowers, scarlet beebalm is well suited to ornamental areas, liking rich, moist soil and partial shade. Divide the clump to propagate and replant every third year.

### Sweet bay (*Laurus nobilis*)

Sweet bay trees can be anything from 3ft to 18ft. (90cm–5.5m). Small shrubs are rather tender, especially suffering from harsh winds, and are easily killed by frost. Grow in a warm, sheltered position, or in tubs, which can be taken under cover in winter (although they are then more prone to pests). Once established, sweet bay becomes a tough, medium-sized tree. It can be attractive as a specimen if trimmed into shape. Sweet bay is difficult to propagate.

### Sweet fennel (*Foeniculum vulgare*)

An upright, stately plant, to 5ft. (1.5m), sweet fennel can be grown in ornamental areas—the bronze form (*F. v.* 'Purpureum') is particularly attractive. It likes an open, sunny position. Propagate the green form from seed or both by division in spring. Replant clumps 2ft. (60cm) apart. It self-seeds readily, so remove flowerheads as they fade if you don't want it coming up everywhere. The flowerheads will attract flower flies.

### Thyme (*Thymus*)

Thyme is low-growing, to 8in. (20cm), so goes well under fruit trees and bushes if it is sunny enough. Thymes will thrive in poor, dry situations and can be grown from seeds or propagated from cuttings. There are many forms, with a range of scents, colors, and shapes, and they can be attractive in ornamental beds. Look out for the caraway-flavored *T. herba-barona* and for the colorful *T. pulegioides* 'Bertram Anderson' (also sometimes sold as 'Anderson's Gold'). The flowers are attractive to bees.

### Winter savory (*Satureja montana*)

Summer savory tastes better but this is shrubbier, to 12in. (30cm), and survives most winters. It grows easily from seed, which should be surface sown and not buried. Plant out in a sunny position and well-drained soil, 9in. (23cm) apart each way. In flower it attracts bees.

# The ornamental garden

Being an organic gardener means, wherever possible, not using anything anywhere that may harm life so we no more want to apply pesticides or herbicides to our lawn and roses than to our cabbages. However, when we think of the ornamental garden our attention changes from production to become more focused on the aesthetics. It's actually very easy to produce usable crops organically but to get a plant to have a perfect appearance is more difficult. To get many plants to do so over the whole year is harder still. That's why people who grow for show often use so many sprays and have to keep doing so to prevent any blemish appearing.

Fortunately we have generally selected our ornamental plants because they are mostly relatively reliable. Only a few of the most highly bred or specialized plants, such as roses, may require much actual pest and disease control. The selection of plants at your local nursery or garden center will mainly consist of those that suffer few problems other than the usual ones of slugs, snails, birds, cats, and the weather!

*Below: Sweet peas, larkspur, and rudbeckia can be grown among the vegetables in the raised beds to create a cottage-garden-style look.*

## Ornamental plants in the organic garden

Most importantly, the wonderful mix of plants with overlapping flowering seasons in the flower garden provides for many more beneficial insects than a vegetable garden or orchard. Furthermore the mixing of such widely diverse plants makes it hard for any pest or disease to spread widely. (The various rusts and mildews and even most aphids that appear on many garden plants at about the same time are not moving from one to the other but are different strains appearing because the conditions in general suit them.)

Lawns are generally a monocrop and so need more care, but, if treated as a rough turfgrass with clovers, daisies, thymes, and chamomile all mixed in, will become much healthier, need less attention, and be more interesting—especially for children.

# Ecology in the ornamental garden

Balancing the physical niches and habitats we can fit into ornamental gardens, from coarse mulches, dense groundcover, beehives, and water features to bird houses and dovecotes, also enables more forms of life to prosper. Thus there is usually ample fertility and rarely do most ornamental areas need additional feeding other than mulches. Indeed they can often be robbed of leaves, grass clippings, and prunings to feed the productive areas. Ideally of course the ornamental garden is near the vegetable garden so the beneficial insects can also benefit the crops.

There is a fashion for growing native and imported wild plants which is fine if these are from reputable growers but we must be careful not to deplete wild stocks to fill our gardens. This especially applies to wild bulbs but many other plants, and even materials such as water-washed limestone rocks, are going the way of extinct animals.

> The wonderful mix of plants in a flower garden provides many more beneficial insects than a vegetable garden

*Below: A rampant honeysuckle creates a natural arch over a path bordered by daphne and ferns, enticing any wandering explorer to creep through.*

*Below: Single-color combinations like this one work well, partly because they highlight the shape and form of the blooms and leaves of each plant.*

# Organic lawn care

Lawns and grass paths make up much of the typical garden. The uniform green shows off plants to perfection, but these areas take a lot of work and cash to maintain.

If you have a small garden think carefully about dispensing with grass altogether: this will not only do away with the lawn mower and the need to have somewhere to store it but will also liberate ground space for more interesting plants. Areas for sitting or sunbathing could be hard-surfaced or graveled instead and surrounded or patch-planted with low-growing plants such as chamomile and thymes.

In a large garden grass is the most sensible groundcover. It is relatively easy to keep neat and tidy, even if it is rather time-consuming. Grassed areas can be established in three ways: by seeding, by sodding, and by cutting the natural cover regularly.

## Seed

Sowing is not expensive, but it is quite hard work. The area must be dug, weeded, leveled, and raked to make a seedbed, and all stones and trash removed. Incorporate ground rock dusts, ground seaweed, and lime or calcified seaweed, to enrich the soil. The first flushes of weeds can be raked or flame-gunned to remove them. The area is then sown in spring or fall with grass seed.

> Sow a mixture of plants such as chamomile and daisies with grass

Tough-wearing recreational ryegrass mixtures are a better choice than the less competitive fine grasses, which look good but do not take hard wear. The fine grasses also prefer acidic conditions, which encourage mosses and weeds.

Sow a mixture of companion plants with the grass, such as clovers, chamomile, creeping thyme, daisies, and yarrow. The mixtures are more interesting and ecologically sound, as well as staying greener when there is a drought. After sowing, rake in the seed, firm it down, and hang up bird scarers. Give the young grass a cut and roll when it is 2in. (5cm) high and keep the usage light for a growing season.

## Sod

Although it is the most expensive way to grass an area, it requires less work than seeding and gives more rapid results. It can only be done well early in spring or fall with damp conditions and/or frequent watering. The area still needs to be dug, enriched, and leveled, but much less thoroughly. Stubborn perennial weeds, like dandelions, must be dug out, but annual weeds can be ignored as they will mostly be killed.

Gardeners should be aware that much sod comes from old meadowland and is frequently pretreated with inorganic fertilizers and herbicides.

## Natural cover

Cutting the natural groundcover regularly is a slow method of getting a good turfgrass, but it produces the most ecologically balanced mixture of plants with the minimum of work and expense. The process is the same as for regularly maintaining or improving an existing lawn, and consists of making the conditions suitable for grasses and unsuitable for most other plants.

If the area is initially too rough for a mower, use a weed whacker for the first cuts. Once the growth is down to rough turfgrass, keep cutting once a week from early spring to late fall, returning the clippings and slowly reducing the height of cut. This kills almost all tall weeds. Acidic-loving weeds are discouraged, and tougher grasses can be aided by liming twice a year with calcified seaweed or dolomitic lime. Patches of clover, which stand out green in a drought, are blended in by sowing clover seed in the remaining areas: clovers improve the lushness of the turfgrass.

# Dethatching

In fall or spring use a wire rake to dethatch the lawn. This is hard work but benefits the lawn. Dethatching produces a mass of thatch for use as a mulch or for composting, but this needs to be moistened with liquid feed to rot down quickly. Follow dethatching by raking in a mixture of ground seaweed, rock dusts and grass seed (with builder's sand for heavy soils), and calcified seaweed. This same feed can be used each spring, but it is better to use diluted urine sprinkled over the turfgrass. It is absorbed rapidly, giving lush growth.

Rosette weeds, such as plantains and thistles, may survive dethatching, cutting, and soil amendment treatments, but they can be hand-pulled with a sharp knife, severing deep underneath to stop regrowth.

# Cutting

Regular cutting is an effective weed-control measure, best done with a rotary mower that can collect the clippings. Reel mowers are not as good in damp conditions or with longer growths. Mowers that leave the clippings build up too much thatch.

Ideally, cut the grass once a week, but vary the height through the season to control growth. The first and last cuts should be high: 2–3in. (5–8cm). Return the clippings to the surface as worms are actively eating them in spring and fall. The spring cuts should decrease in height to 1–1¼in. (2–3cm) by midspring, and remain there until midsummer, removing and returning the clippings alternately.

From midsummer raise the height to 1¼–2in. (3–5cm) to keep the grass greener and more drought-resistant, and then to 2–3in. (5–8cm) from late fall, removing the clippings until the last leaves fall. Keep the mower blades sharp to make the job easier.

# Awkward spots

A string trimmer can do the edges and around tree trunks and get into awkward and difficult spots. It is also good for trimming grass to different heights. Either side of a mown path in a wild area or orchard, for example, the grass can be kept about 12in. (30cm) high, so it does not fall over the path. Cutting grass with a string trimmer can provide a good environment for bulbs, primroses, cowslips, and violets, as the area can be kept neat without becoming overgrown and choking out these little treasures.

# Planning an organic garden

Before you plan your garden it is important to consider what you want from it. Is it to add value to your property, give you an interest in life, impress your friends—or is it just for the exercise? Do you need to provide a play area for children? If you want to grow fruit and vegetables, which ones do you want and when? After all, if you always go on vacation in late summer there is not much point planting early apples. Similarly, do you want to grow flowers for cutting or for outdoor beauty?

## Details

There should be somewhere to sit, but is it to be an outdoor room or will you enjoy a vista from a window? If you want privacy, effective screening may be more important than saving money or maximizing self-sufficiency. Once you know what the parameters are then it is much easier to plan around them. Consider and plan a garden in the same way you would buy a new car or refit the kitchen—and be similarly prepared to spend a realistic amount of money.

> Choose the areas you want for food production first

## Planning on paper

It will help to make a scale plan showing the boundaries, walls, utility pipes, immovable objects (such as fuel tanks), solid paths, trees, major shrubs, and so on, which are difficult to alter. Given time and money anything is possible in garden design, but it is much easier to work around the more permanent features than to alter them. On the other hand, areas of grass, vegetable and ornamental gardens can be moved around or altered at will. Choose the areas you want for food production first, as these need the best sites, then add other areas as space allows.

Looking at the plan will help you to see the garden as a whole, so you can organize it more rationally. Try to get the maximum use out of each item. For example, position a shed so that it shelters a bed and so that the largest blank wall faces the sun: you can then train a fruit bush against it. Position bird houses under the eaves. The overflow from the rain barrels can be fed to a pool.

# Garden features

There are many features that can be added to a garden, in much the same way as doing a house conversion—greenhouse, pond, fruit cage, and so on. You do not have to have conventional front and back yards—you can have your garden any way you like, with vegetables in the front and flowers at the back, or even just have a single, enormous fruit cage or a woodland area full of naturalized bulbs and a pond.

# Getting started: organic dos and don'ts

✓ **Do** recycle all garden and household garbage for compost and reuse.

✓ **Do** maximize the natural system of checks and balances by growing a wide variety of plants.

✓ **Do** create habitats for birds and animals, especially by supplying water in the form of ponds and pools.

✓ **Do** stop using all herbicides. Instead, use the recommended methods of weed control (see pages 50–3), which usually involve no more work and are more pleasant and safer.

✓ **Do** stop using most insecticides, which are rarely necessary, though a few of the least harmful ones can be used as a last resort (see page 31).

✓ **Do** stop using most fungicides (except those described on page 31).

✓ **Do** use companion planting to outmanouver pests and avoid diseases (see pages 66–9).

✗ **Don't** use soluble fertilizers, although they can be used up if greatly diluted and watered onto grass in spring when they will be taken up rapidly with little danger of run-off.

✗ **Don't** use peat.

✗ **Don't** use unecological plants, such as imported wild bulbs and bedding plants.

✗ **Don't** use plastic products when natural or longer-lasting alternatives are available.

*Left: The selection of fragrant thymes planted beneath the log seat make it an especially pleasant place to take a break.*

Herbs are useful, easy to grow, and attractive to beneficial insects, and every garden should have space for at least a few, especially as herbs do not need much space or attention.

## Hard surfaces

One of the most essential areas in any garden is somewhere to sit and relax outside—after all, this is one of the most important aspects of gardening. Hardscaping such as, slabs or even gravel is more practical than grass and takes far less upkeep. A deck or patio must be easily accessible from the house, ideally extending out from a sun room or kitchen, or it will rarely be used.

Patios in sunny positions soak up heat and give early ripening crops of fruit planted around them, especially grapes, which can be wound round posts or over wires. Varieties of creeping thyme and chamomile will grow happily in holes or between slabs and give an exquisite scent when walked on. The patio can be edged with scented plants and aromatic herbs to add more sweet smells and help to discourage flies and mosquitoes. Bird houses fixed to the wall and under the eaves can give extra interest and pest control; a platform bird feeder and birdbath will attract even more birds.

*Below: For most people, flowers are a very important element of garden design. They contribute beauty and charm, and provide nectar and pollen for beneficial insects. The border shows scarlet beebalm and golden feverfew in the front with a pear tree on the right and a mix of phloxes behind.*

# Garden size

Although most of us would prefer a larger garden, it is surprising what can be done even with a tiny one. In a small garden you can produce quantities of fruit, vegetables, and flowers with the same amount of time and effort that in a larger area would be spent just cutting the grass. Moreover, in a small area any money spent is much more effective: you can buy slow-growing evergreen shrubs or build low-maintenance features, such as paved areas, whereas in a larger garden far more investment is needed.

One advantage of a larger garden is the extra privacy, especially if you have room for an informal hedge and windbreak. An extra benefit for the organic gardener is the isolation that comes with a well-hedged garden: spray drift, pests and disease spores from other gardens are less likely to arrive on your plants. In addition, the extra space for plants and habitats means that more forms of beneficial wildlife can be encouraged and retained, aiding pest control.

A large garden also contributes plenty of prunings, grass clippings, and leaves to compost for use in the vegetable garden and elsewhere. With more land the vegetable garden can be less intensively cropped, and longer rotations and green manure will give better crops, less prone to disease. There is also room for

> There is no reason, state laws allowing, why even the smallest garden should not have a chicken or two

livestock which can convert your waste to eggs or meat, and provide a source of high-value fertilizer —although there is no reason, state laws allowing, why even the smallest garden should not have a chicken or two.

## Small urban garden

Gardens in dense urban areas often enjoy greater shelter and warmth than those in more open country. Brickwork, tiles, and paving slabs store heat, while buildings reduce low-level wind. Heat is also produced by people, buildings, and cars, and there are often higher levels of carbon dioxide. All this warmth means that the growing season begins several weeks earlier. The last frost of spring always comes much later in rural areas than it does in the city nearby.

*Below: Hens are worth keeping for the fertility they return to the soil—and, of course, for the eggs.*

Size does not so much limit the kind of garden as the number of internal subdivisions. You cannot sensibly fit a fruit cage, a rose garden, a vegetable garden, a lawn, and a water feature

*Above: A pond provides a valuable habitat for wildlife as well as being attractive in its own right.*

*Below: Beehives work well in a semi-wild area which is set slightly apart from the rest of the garden.*

into a 10 x 10ft. (3 x 3m) yard. However, you could make a beautiful and productive combination from a couple of these features. So concentrate on one or two of the options rather than trying to squeeze in as many as you can.

Even the tiniest yard has room for herbs, in pots and containers if not a whole bed of them, and where there is space a salad bed gives valuable returns. A patio area is much better value in all weather conditions than a small piece of grass. With scented plants and a small pond, you can create a tranquil little retreat from the hurly-burly of life. Fruit can be grown trained on walls and as screens, or even in large pots or containers. There may be room for a small vegetable garden or an ornamental area with productive plants.

There is always room for a compost bin and even for bees. Beekeeping is ideal for urban gardeners—bees add life and interest to the garden, are productive, and thrive on the longer, milder seasons and wide range of urban plants. They are more productive the more attention they receive, so are ideal if you have a small garden and plenty of spare time. Bird houses and food for birds can also be squeezed into the tiniest yards.

## Larger urban garden

For most people the typical garden is divided up into several areas, often with a fairly formal front garden and enough space to produce significant amounts of fruit and vegetables if well planned. This is, perhaps, the optimum size for most gardeners without much spare time, as the entire area can be kept attractive and productive without extra help. The larger garden does need careful planning and good routines, because otherwise too many chores eat into the time. Provided the work is organized so that it is spread over a few hours a week rather than being left so that the garden becomes unmanageable, it is possible to keep everything under control.

There should certainly be room for a fruit cage, greenhouse, vegetable garden, and fruit trees, which are best placed as far from the house as practicable. Ornamental areas with lawns, deck or patio, a pool, and the herb garden should be as near as possible to the house for convenience.

When deciding on other features, it is probably better to concentrate on a few, rather than trying to cram them all in. That way, each can have sufficient space to be worthwhile. For example, it may be preferable to have grapevines or an asparagus bed but not both.

## Large rural garden

If you have up to 1 acre (4,000 square meters), what and how you grow is mainly limited by time and money, but then the garden needs either rigorous planning and/or ruthless maintenance or hired labor. I have squeezed more and more into my rural garden, but it does take up the equivalent of every weekend throughout the year to stay on top of it. This is the optimum size for a keen gardener—any larger and it needs to be simplified in many areas or you need help.

Intensive methods are better replaced with extensive ones—semi-dwarf trees in a grassed orchard rather than trained cordons; vegetables on the flat instead of in raised beds; fewer, bigger, more shrubby areas with sweeping curves and less edging. Grass cutting is effective for maintaining

large areas neatly but is one of the most time-consuming chores, and it may be a good idea to hire labor for this rather than for the more enjoyable work.

Ease of access, good pathways, and locating the least visited areas farthest away are vitally important—a lot of time can be wasted going backwards and forwards to fetch tools. The space available allows for a wide range of wildlife habitats, as well as a hen run and a small pond. A garden this size should be self-sufficient in fertility.

## Very large rural garden

With 2.5 acres (1 hectare) or more, almost any garden imaginable can be created. You could certainly become self-sufficient in fruit and vegetables, and would be able to keep whatever livestock you have time for. In order to minimize labor, large areas need to be simplified, grassed and cut with a string trimmer regularly, enabling you to feed the rest of the garden with clippings as mulch and fertility.

> Without careful planning, too much space could prove more of a curse than a blessing

Machinery and hired labor become a necessity for many more of the tasks, although four-legged lawn mowers can replace this to a great extent. Gardening as such becomes landscaping around the house, and a large garden becomes more of a larger urban garden with a couple of acres of pasture or private woodland extending out from it. Without careful planning, too much space could prove more of a curse than a blessing!

# Garden plans

With planning, even the tiniest yard can incorporate several organic features. The two plans here should give you some good ideas. The small backyard is 32ft x 26ft. (10m x 8m) and the large one is 68ft x 46ft. (21m x 14m). Both are thickly planted or mulched.

**Small backyard, south facing**

1 **Worm compost bins** are particularly ideal for small gardens and can be tucked away in shady corners.

2 **Rain barrels**, fed from house gutters, are connected to each other with siphons to multiply capacity. In the large yard, rain barrels can also be located near the greenhouse.

3 **Herb bed** needs plenty of air and light.

4 **Vegetable garden** needs full light and air. Each bed is roughly 1yd (1m) wide with concrete stepping-stone paths between them to save space. It is aligned north to south to catch maximum sun.

5 **Ornamental fruit cage**, painted black and decorated with finials. This is both attractive and practical.

6 **Small greenhouse**. This is the best value use of your garden space. Whether it is a lean-to against a south-facing wall or free-standing, it will need full sun. An ideal site is next to the house so that you can make use of the house's central heating system.

7 **Larger greenhouse** located at the end of the garden in full sun.

8 **Small pool**, with sloping rough edges, one of mud, to allow wildlife easy access to the pool. A metal safety grille should be fitted just beneath the water surface to make the pool safe for children.

9 **Large pond**, to allow you more scope for attracting wildlife.

10 **Bird houses**. Find space for as many as possible on walls, under eaves, and in every dense shrub and evergreen.

11 **Ladybeetle and lacewing nests**. Attract these beneficial insects with bundles of hollow stems and sticks hidden in dry nooks.

12 **Rotting logs** form part of the pool habitat for beetles and dragonflies and cover pots that have been buried to provide homes for frogs and toads.

13 **Pile of stones, tiles, plates, and bottles**, well hidden under evergreen shrubs and well away from the vegetables, provides a habitat to encourage other small creatures.

**Large backyard, south facing**

**14 Cordon or espalier apples** create a screen and allow you to fit more varieties into a small space. These will need supports and careful pruning.

**15 Tree removed.** In a small garden any tree takes too much light and space and should go unless it is productive, protected, or much loved.

**16 Lawn removed** so that all space is either productive or ornamental and there is no need for a lawn mower or for storage for one.

**17 Fence covered with vines** to soften and disguise boundaries and optimize planting space.

**18 Thickly planted and mulched,** with small stepping stones as pathways.

# A year in the garden—Spring

| | Plant | Sow | Feed | Mulch | Spray | Prune |
|---|---|---|---|---|---|---|
| **Early spring** | Artichokes, asparagus, garlic, onion sets, potatoes, and shallots<br><br>Evergreen shrubs and trees | Under hoop houses: beet, black salsify, cabbages, cauliflowers, carrots, chards, fava beans, herbs, kohlrabi, leeks, lettuces, parsnips, peas, radishes, salsify, scallions, spinach, and turnips; sweet peas | Spring greens with comfrey liquid or seaweed solution | Spread everywhere | Everything with diluted seaweed solution | Evergreens and conifer hedges<br>...................<br>Hollow-stemmed and borderline hardy shrubs |
| **Midspring** | Onion seedlings and potato sets<br>...................<br>Perennial herbs<br>...................<br>Evergreen trees and shrubs | Under hoop houses: beans (dwarf, fava, pole), black salsify, brassicas (most), carrots, fennel, kohlrabi, leeks, lettuces and salad greens, parsnips, peas, radishes, rutabagas and turnips; salsify, spinach; herbs; sweet peas | | Spread everywhere | Everything with diluted seaweed solution | Early-flowering shrubs as flowers fade<br>...................<br>Remove seedheads from bulbs as they die back |
| **Late spring** | Corn, cucumbers, zucchini and summer squash | Under hoop houses: corn, cucumbers, melons, pumpkins, tomatoes, and zucchini and summer squash; half-hardy flowers<br>...................<br>In the open: beans (dwarf, fava, pole), black salsify, brassicas (most), carrots, fennel, kohlrabi, leeks, lettuces and salad greens, parsnips, peas, radishes, rutabagas and turnips; salsify, spinach; herbs; sweet peas and wallflowers | Tomatoes and pot plants with comfrey liquid or seaweed solution<br>...................<br>Incorporate compost with all transplants | Spread under and around potatoes | Everything with diluted seaweed solution | Early-flowering shrubs as flowers fade |

# Spring

| | Fruit | Routine tasks | In the greenhouse | Lawns and grass | Containers | General | |
|---|---|---|---|---|---|---|---|
| | Remove old canes of fall-fruiting raspberries<br><br>Spray peaches and almonds with Bordeaux mixture<br><br>Plant grapevines, soft fruit, and rhubarb | Compost, dig in, or invert green manures | Sow cucumbers, eggplants, peppers, and tomatoes | Feed with sifted compost or seaweed solution<br><br>Cut weekly once in growth, leaving clippings<br><br>Move, lay, and repair sod | | Protect early flowers and buds against frost<br><br>Replace sticky bands if necessary | **Early spring** |
| | | Weed regularly | Sow corn, cucumbers, melons, pumpkins, tomatoes, and zucchini and summer squash<br><br>Sow half-hardy flowers | Cut weekly<br><br>Use clippings for mulch | Topdress permanent plantings | Put down slug pubs<br><br>Look for signs of pests and diseases<br><br>Check sticky bands<br><br>Protect tender flowers, fruitlets, and plantlets against frost | **Midspring** |
| | Remove badly placed and overcrowded branches on apricots and peaches | Weed regularly<br><br>Water fall and spring plantings | | Cut weekly<br><br>Use clippings for mulch | | Tie in and support vines and tall herbaceous plants<br><br>Put down slug pubs<br><br>Check sticky bands<br><br>Look for signs of pests (especially aphids, cabbage white caterpillars, and spider mites) and diseases<br><br>Protect flowers, fruitlets, and plants against late frosts | **Late spring** |

# A year in the garden—Summer

| | Plant | Sow | Feed | Mulch | Spray | Prune |
|---|---|---|---|---|---|---|
| **Early summer** | Transplant brassicas and leeks | Beet, chicory, endive, kohlrabi, lettuces and salad greens, rutabagas and turnips, spinach; biennial and perennial flowers | Tomatoes and pot plants with comfrey liquid or seaweed solution <br><br> Incorporate compost with all transplants | Spread under and around potatoes | Everything with diluted seaweed solution | Deadhead and cut back most flowering shrubs as flowers fade |
| **Midsummer** | Potato sets for late crop | Carrots, chards, Chinese cabbages, kohlrabi, lettuces and salad greens, rutabagas, turnips, and winter spinach | Incorporate compost with potato sets | | Everything with diluted seaweed solution <br><br> Maincrop potatoes with Bordeaux mixture in warm, humid weather | Evergreens and conifer hedges <br><br> Deadhead regularly |
| **Late summer** | Daffodil bulbs | Japanese onions, scallions, winter lettuces and salad greens, and winter spinach <br><br> Green manures as soil becomes vacant | | | Everything with diluted seaweed solution | |

# Summer

| Fruit | Rountine tasks | In the greenhouse | Lawns and grass | Con-tainers | General | |
|-------|---------------|-------------------|-----------------|-------------|---------|---|
| Summer prune grapes<br>Protect fruit from birds<br>Thin, harvest, and use ripening fruit | Weed regularly<br>Water as required | | Cut weekly | | Check sticky bands<br>Look for signs of pests (especially aphids, caterpillars, and spider mites) and diseases | Early summer |
| Prune plums and flowering and fruiting cherries<br>Summer prune apple and pear trees<br>Prune red- and white-currants and grapevines<br>Protect fruit from birds<br>Thin, harvest, and use ripening fruit | Weed regularly<br>Water as required | | Cut as necessary<br>Use clippings for mulch | | Check sticky bands<br>Looks for signs of pests and diseases<br>Protect fruit from birds<br>Put down water for birds | Midsummer |
| Cut out old blackcurrant stems after fruiting<br>Transplant strawberry runners<br>Protect fruit from birds<br>Thin, harvest, and use ripening fruit | Weed regularly<br>Water as required | | Cut as necessary<br>Use clippings for mulch | | Order hardy trees and shrubs for fall planting<br>Clean, paint, and repair timber, gutters, and brickwork<br>Put down water for birds | Late summer |

# A year in the garden—Fall

| | Plant | Sow | Feed | Mulch | Spray | Prune |
|---|---|---|---|---|---|---|
| **Early fall** | Garlic and other bulbs<br><br>Transplant biennial flowering plants | Under hoop houses: Chinese greens, early carrots, turnips, salad greens, and winter lettuces<br><br>In the open: green manure | Incorporate compost with all transplants | Rake over old mulch | Everything with diluted seaweed solution | Herbaceous plants to 6in. (15cm) as growth fades |
| **Midfall** | Deciduous trees and shrubs | Sow summer cauliflowers, salad greens, and winter lettuces; sweet peas; green manures | Incorporate compost with all plantings<br><br>Spread sifted compost around trees, shrubs, and soft fruit | Spread new mulch everywhere | | Herbaceous plants to 6in. (15cm) as growth fades<br><br>Late-flowering shrubs as leaves fall |
| **Late fall** | Deciduous shrubs and trees | Hardy fava beans and peas | Incorporate compost with all plantings<br><br>Spread compost over asparagus and globe artichokes | | | Herbaceous plants to 6in. (15cm) as growth fades<br><br>Late-flowering shrubs as leaves fall |

| Fruit | Routine tasks | In the greenhouse | Lawns and grass | Con-tainers | General | |
|---|---|---|---|---|---|---|
| Remove old raspberry and blackberry canes and tie in new ones<br><br>Harvest and use or store | Weed regularly<br><br>Lift and store dahlias and gladioli<br><br>Take cuttings of woody plants before leaves drop | | Cut as necessary<br><br>Use clippings for mulch | | Collect and store seed<br><br>Check sticky bands<br><br>Protect fruit and flowers from early frost<br><br>Search for pests | Early fall |
| Prune soft fruit and grapevines as the leaves fall<br><br>Remove old raspberry and blackberry canes and tie in new ones<br><br>Plant new soft fruit<br><br>Harvest and use or store<br><br>Put cloches over fall strawberries | Weed regularly<br><br>Lift and divide hardy herbaceous plants and rhubarb<br><br>Make new beds and borders<br><br>Put cloches over salad plants | | Cut weekly, raising height of blade<br><br>Leave clippings with shredded leaves or collect and use for mulch | Move indoors or under shelter | Collect and store seeds and berries<br><br>Check sticky bands<br><br>Protect borderline hardy plants against frost<br><br>Turn compost piles and cover<br><br>Sieve well-rotted compost so it is ready for use | Midfall |
| Winter prune apple, pears, and nonstone fruit<br><br>Plant soft fruit<br><br>Harvest and store last fruit | Weed regularly<br><br>In cold gardens lift and store root vegetables | | Cut as necessary<br><br>Collect clippings and use with leaves for mulch | | Check sticky bands<br><br>Order seed catalogs, potatoes, and herbaceous plants for spring<br><br>Collect waste for composting or shredding | Late fall |

# A year in the garden—Winter

| | Plant | Sow | Feed | Mulch | Spray | Prune |
|---|---|---|---|---|---|---|
| **Early winter** | Deciduous trees and shrubs | | Incorporate compost with all plantings<br><br>Spread compost over the crowns of herbaceous plants | | | Late-flowering shrubs as leaves fall |
| **Midwinter** | Chit potato seed in a light, frost-free place | | Every few years spread lime or calcified seaweed over soil | | | Remove any damaged or diseased growth |
| **Late winter** | Garlic, onion sets, and shallots<br><br>Trees and shrubs | | Spread seaweed on bare soil and mulches and rake in | | Outdoor peaches and almonds with Bordeaux mixture | Remove any damaged or diseased growth |

# Winter

| Fruit | Routine tasks | In the greenhouse | Lawns and grass | Con-tainers | General | |
|-------|---------------|-------------------|-----------------|-------------|---------|---|
| Prune soft fruit and grapevines as leaves fall<br><br>Winter prune apples, pears, and nonstone fruit<br><br>Plant soft fruit | Weed as necessary<br><br>In mild gardens harvest and store root vegetables | Clean all glass and surfaces | Lime, aerate, and spike, adding builder's sand, if needed | | Check sticky bands<br><br>Clean cloches, hoop houses, and cold frames<br><br>Clean out gutters and drains when last leaves have fallen | Early winter |
| | Dig new beds | | | | Plan and make changes<br><br>Order seed<br><br>Put out food for birds | Midwinter |
| Plant soft fruit<br><br>Pick off big buds on blackcurrants | Set out cloches, hoop houses, and plastic sheet mulches to warm up soil | Sow cabbages, carrots, cauliflowers, early peas, fava beans, indoor tomatoes, lettuces, potatoes, radishes, spinach and turnips<br><br>In pots: onions and scallions; sweet peas | Spread seaweed and rake in<br><br>In mild weather cut with blade set high and leave clippings | | Sift and mix home-made potting soils<br><br>Top up indoor beds with compost<br><br>Inspect ties, stakes, and labels on woody plants<br><br>Firm roots of fall planting after the last frosts<br><br>Check sticky bands<br><br>Empty insect traps and nests | Late winter |

# Index

Page numbers in *italic* refer to illustrations

### A
acidity, soil 6, 9
air, soil 8
alfalfa 18
alkaline soils 6
alliums (onions) 21, 65, 67, 68, 94–5
almonds 109
amending soil 6–7
American gooseberry mildew 44, *44*
anise 117
annual meadow grass *59*
ants 36
aphids 33, 34, 36, 38, *38, 77*
apple canker 44, *44*
apple of Peru *87*
apple sawflies 38, *38*
apples 108–9, *108*, 131
arugula 114–5
asparagus 65, 102
asparagus beetle 38, *38*
asparagus peas 101

### B
bacterial canker 44, *44*
balanced organic fertilizers 16
bands 35, 36
basalt 16
basil 115

beans 18, 65, 99–100
beehives *128*
beet 67, 90, *90*
beneficial insects 77–9
*Berberis thunbergii 80*
big bud mites 38, *38*
biological control 33
birds 34, 80–1
  scarers 37
bishop's weed *61*
bitter dock *60*
blackberries 111
blackcurrants 65, 111–12, *111*
blackfly *38*, 39
blackleg 45, *45*
black salsify 93
block planting 82–3
bone meal 15
borage 115, *115*
Bordeaux mixture 31
botrytis 45, *45*
brassicas 21, 67, 95–8
broccoli 65, 96, *98*
broccoli raab 65, 96, *96*
brussels spouts 65, 96
buckwheat 18, *20*, 21
*Buddleja 75, 77*
bush beans 99–100
buttercup *61*

### C
cabbage root fly 34, 39, *39*
cabbages 67, 96, *97*
calcified seaweed 15

calcium 21
caraway 115
cardboard mulches 56
carpet squares 34–5
carrot rust flies 34, 39, *39*
carrots 65, 67, 90–1, *90*
catnip 68
caterpillars 33, 34, 39, *39*
cauliflowers 97, *97*
celandine *60*
celeriac 67, 102
celery 67, 102
chamomile 69
chard 67, 99
chervil 115
chicory 18, 21, 98–9
chickweed 21
children 37
chili peppers 106
Chinese cabbage 97
chives 68, 69, 117
clay soils 9, 10
clover 18
clubroot 45, *45*
cocoa shells 56
codling moths 35, 39, *39*
coir 13
comfrey liquid 16–17, *17*
common balm 117, *118*
companion planting 66–9
compost (garden) 12, 13
  activators 22
  containers *24*, 25
  easy 29

making 22–9
materials 26–7
turning 24
worms 29
composted bark 13, 56
containers 88–9
copper tape 37
coriander 115, *115*
corn *11*, 65, 67, 100
corn marigold 21
corn salad 19
creeping thistle *61*
cucumber mosaic 46, *46*
cucumbers 65, 67, 105–6
cumin 115
cutworms 40, *40*

D
damping off 46, *46*
damsons 110–11
dandelion 21, *61*
derris 31
dethatching lawns 123
digging 10–11, 52
dill 116
diseases 70
  controlling 44–9
  resistant plants 64–5
docks *60*
drainage 10
dwarf beans 67, 100, *100*

E
earwigs 35, 36, 40, *40*

ecology, ornamental gardens 121
eggplants *104*, 105
endives 98–9
European plum 110–11
Europe sage 116

F
fava beans 67, 99, 100–1
fennel 103
fenugreek 18
fertility, soil 12
fertilizers 14–15
feverfew *32*, 68, 117, *126*
fireblight 46, *46*
fish emulsion 17
flame-gunning 53
flea beetles 34, 40, *40*
flowering tobaccos 21
fodder radish 19
foxgloves *74, 77*
French marigolds, 68
fruit 108–13
  containers 88–9
  greenhouses 86
fungus gnat 33

G
garden lovage 117
garden peas 101
garlic 67, 68, 69, 94, *94*
German chamomile 21
globe artichokes 103, *103*

golden feverfew *32*, 68, 117, *126*
gooseberries 65, 112, *112*
goosegrass, 21
grapes 65
grapevines *64, 89*
gravel 56
green manure 18–20
greenhouses 84–7, 130
grit 13
ground rock basalt 16
ground rock phosphate 16
ground rock potassium 15–16
groundcover 51
groundsel *59*

H
hairy bittercress *59*
handweeding 53
heliotrope *61*
herbs 114–19
  containers 88
hoeing 53
honeysuckle *121*
hoof and horn 15
hoop houses 84–6, *85*
horseradish *60*, 117
horsetails 21, *61*
Hungarian grazing rye 19
hybrid berries 111
hygiene 32, 52

I
insecticidal soap 31
ivy *51*

J
Japanese knotweed *60*
Jerusalem artichokes 91
jimson weed 21

K
kale *97*, 98
kohlrabi 91, *91*

L
lacewings 76, 130
ladybeetles 76, 130
lamb's quarters 21
larkspur *120*
lavender 68, 117, *118*
lawns 122–3
leaf spot 46, *46*
leafmold 13, 26, *26, 28*, 56
leatherjackets 40, *40*
leeks 65, 67, 94
lemon beebrush 117–8
lettuces 65, 67, 98–9
lime 7
*Limnanthes douglasii* 19, *20, 69*
liquid fertilizers 16–17
loam 9, 13
lucerne 18
lupines 19
lures 36

M
manure 13, 17
  green 18–20
marigold 68, 116

marjoram 118
mealybugs 33, 40, *40*
melons 21, 65, 67
mice 37
microclimates 63
mildew 47, *47*
minerals 21
mint *51*, 118
mowing lawns 123
mulching 54–7, *55, 56*
municipal wastes 13
mustard 19

N
nasturtiums 68, *68*
nectarines 109
nets, pests 34
nettle tea 16–17
nettles 21, *28*, 61, 68
*Nicotiana sylvestris 85*
nitrogen 14, 21
no-dig methods 10

O
okra 102
onion flies 41, *41*
onions 21, 65, 67, 68, 94–5
organic material 8, 12
ornamental garden 120–1

P
paper mulches 56
parsley *32*, 116, *116*
parsnips 65, 92

paths *71, 121*
pea moths 41, *41*
pea weevils 41, *41*
peach leaf curl 47, *47*
peaches 109, *109*
pear midges 34, 41, *41*
pears 110
peas *11*, 18, 65, 67, 101
peat 12
peat soils 9
peppers 65, 105, *106*
pests 70
  controlling 30–43
pH 7
*Phacelia tanacetifolia* 19
phlox *126*
phosphate 16
phosphorus 14, 21
planning 124–31
plantain 21
plants
  basic care 70–1
  choosing 62–73
  companion 66–9
  disease resistant 64–5
  watering 72–3
plastic mulches 56
plum fruit moths 35
plums 110–11, *110*
pole beans *15*, 67, 101–2
ponds 75, *75, 128*, 130
potassium 14, 16, 21
potato blight 47, *47*
potatoes *11*, 65, 67, 92–3

potting mixes 13
primroses *51*
prunings, mulches 56
pumpkins 67, 104–5, *105*
purslane 21
pyrethrum 31

Q
quackgrass *61*
quassia 31

R
radishes 93
raised beds 83
raspberries 65, 112–13, *113*
raspberry beetles 34, 41, *41*
redcurrants 113, *113*
reversion disease 48, *48*
rhododendrons *7*
rose black spot 48, *48*
rosemary *32*, 118, *119*
roses *71*
rotary cultivating 52–3
rotation 70, 82
row planting 82–3
rudbeckia *120*
rust 48, *48*
rutabagas 65, 67, 93
rye 19

S
sacrificial crops 66
sage 118, *119*
salsify 93

sand mulches 56
sandy soils 9, 13
sawflies 35, 38
scab 49, *49*
scale insects 42, *42*
scarlet beebalm 119, *126*
sea kale 103–4, *103*
seaweed 14, 15, 17
  sprays 71
semi-permeable membranes 57
sempervivums *32*
sewage sludge 16
shady positions 63
shallots 94
shepherd's purse 21, *59*
silica 21
silt soils 9
silverleaf 49, *49*
slugs 33, 34, 36, 37
snails 34, 36
snap peas 101
snow peas 101
sod 122
soft rot 49, *49*
soft soap 31
soil
  acidic 6
  amending 6–7
  analysis 7
  digging 10–11
  drainage 10
  fertility 12–13
  types 8–9, 62
  understanding 6

spider mites 33, 42, *42*
spinach 65, 99
squashes 67, 104–5
stem worms 42, *42*
sticky traps 35, 36
stinging nettle 16–17, 21, *28*,
  *61*, 68
stony soil 9
straw mulches 56
strawberries *15*, 113
string trimmer 123
sulfur 21, 31
summer savory 116, *116*
summer squashes 65, 67, 106
sunny positions 63
sweet bay 119
sweet fennel 119
sweet peas *120*
sweet peppers 106, *106*
Swiss chard 99

T
tayberry 5
thistles *61*
thrips 33, 35, *85*
thyme *72*, 119, *125*
tomatoes *64*, 65, 67, 106–7,
  *107*
trefoil 19
turnip-rooted parsley 92
turnips 67, 93, *93*

U
urine 28

V
*Valerianella* 19
vegetables 90–107
  containers 88
  gardens 82–3
  greenhouses 84–7
  raised beds 83
vetches 21
vine weevils 33, 42, *42*

W
wasps 35, 43, *43*
water, soil 8

water features 75, *75*
watering 72–3
waterlogged soils 10
weeds, controlling 50–*61*
whitecurrants 113
whiteflies 33, 34, 35, 43, *43, 85, 87*
wildlife, encouraging 74–81
winter moth 36
winter savory 119
winter squashes 106
winter tares 19
wireworms 36, 43, *43*

wood ash 16
wood chip mulches 56
wooly aphids 43, *43*
worms 8
  composting 29, 130

Z
zucchini 65, 104–5, *104*

# Acknowledgments

All photography by Jerry Harpur except for the following listed below:
Garden Picture Library/David Cavagnaro 93
Holt Studios/Nigel Cattlin 28 left/Andy Morant 24
Leigh Jones 26
Octopus Publishing Group Limited 89 left/Mark Bolton 56/Michael Boyes 68/Dave Jordan front cover, back cover top/Peter Myers 28 right/George Wright 7, 80

Plant Illustrations Susan Hillier
Garden Plans Cactus Design

Editorial Manager Jane Birch
Executive Art Editor Leigh Jones
Designer Peter Crump
Picture Researcher Jennifer Veall
Production Controller Lucy Woodhead